DATE DUE

DEMCO 38-296

CHINA'S LEGAL SYSTEM

A General Survey

Du Xichuan   Zhang Lingyuan

NEW WORLD PRESS   BEIJING CHINA

First Edition 1990

ISBN: 7-80005-087-4

Published by
NEW WORLD PRESS
24 Baiwanzhuang Road, Beijing, 100037, China

Distributed by
CHINA INTERNATIONAL BOOK TRADING CORPORATION
21 Chegongzhuang Xilu, Beijing, China
P.O. Box 399, Beijing, China   Postal Zone: 100044

Printed in the People's Republic of China

Preface

China's policy of opening to the outside world creates broad opportunities for the Chinese and other people to exchange information and cooperate in every cultural, political, economic, scientific and technological sphere. China, under its new "open policy," stresses the understanding and study of the legal systems of other societies. Likewise, many friends from abroad may want to study, and become familiar with, both the present status of China's legal system, and the directions in which it is developing.

China's legal system has a long and complex history. It gradually began to form as early as the time of slave society. During an extended historical period, this nascent legal system underwent continuous development and change. Since the founding of the People's Republic of China, particularly within the past several years, China's legal system changed considerably as the creation of a distinctly Chinese and socialist legal system moved toward completion. The successive drafting and promulgation of the Chinese Constitution, the general principles of civil law, civil prosecution law, criminal law, criminal prosecution law, patent law, trademark law, economic contract law, foreign economic contract law, the law on foreign investment enterprises, joint venture law, enterprise bankruptcy law, the law governing the exit and entry of Chinese citizens, the law governing the exit and entry of

3

foreigners, plus over fifty other major laws, have created a favorable legal climate for foreigners to invest, work and travel in China. The introduction of China's legislative and judicial systems, as well as its basic principles, to foreign friends by Chinese legal specialists, therefore, is urgently needed.

China's Legal System: A General Survey co—written by Du Xichuan and Zhang Lingyuan includes the following information: a briefing on the development of laws in China, China's legislative bodies, legislative procedure, judicial bodies and procedure, procuratorial bodies, public security and policy bodies, institutions of administration of justice, lawyers notarial institutions and China's civil and criminal law systems and economic laws concerning foreign enterprises.

This book is helpful in understanding and doing research on China's legal system.

Zhang Youyu
Member of the Sixth NPC Standing
Committee and its Law Committee,
advisor of the Law Committee of the
Seventh NPC Standing Committee,
and honorary president of All-China
Lawyers Association

March 1987

Contents

CHAPTER *1*

Establishment and Development of China's Legal System

The building of democracy and legal system in China has followed a long and tortuous course of development. More than thirty years have passed since New China launched its legal system. Today, China's legal system is capturing wide attention. The Chinese people have looked back at their history of social development and have learned a painful lesson from the ten-year catastrophe of the "cultural revolution." They have thus come to a definite conclusion: To achieve socialist modernization, China must improve and perfect its legal system on a basis of democracy. Economic and legal developments must go hand in hand.

PREPARATORY PERIOD FOR BUILDING A PEOPLE'S DEMOCRATIC LEGAL SYSTEM

Sprawling across the continent of Asia, China is a home of early mankind and ancient civilization. In the 21st century B.C., China was a slave-owning society with a corresponding legal system. Feudalism was established in 475 B.C.; at this time, China's feudal society and legal system began their meandering development. Chinese feudal laws, from the first statutory law, *The Legal Classics*, [1] to the last legal code, *The Great Qing*

---

[1] The first systematic feudal code in Chinese history. Written in the early Warring States Period, it was basically composed of criminal law and criminal procedure law.

Dynasty Law, [1] have similar concepts, but viewed in sequence, they also reveal a slow process of historical change and development. Starting from the early 7th century, China's feudal legal system began to have an impact on the legal systems of its neighboring countries including Japan, Korea, and Vietnam. This eventually resulted in a set of legal systems with world-wide influence.

However, with China's long history of a self-sufficient natural economy, its laws began to fall behind those of other countries, especially in the newly developing Western world. China's feudal society was not amenable to progress in the legal realm, because autocratic monarchy and dictatorship prevailed and the legal system was merely an ornament or tool for the harsh rule of the feudal leaders.

A socialist legal system in China depended upon development of the national democratic movement, social, political, and economic progress, and growing moral consciousness of the people for its foundation. Such a legal system was established and gradually improved after the People's War of Liberation (August 1945-September 1949), in which the Chinese people won their struggle against imperialism and feudalism and subsequently founded the People's Republic of China in 1949. The Chinese people, led by the Communist Party of China (CPC), smashed the military offensives of the Kuomintang (KMT) and overthrew the KMT dictatorial rule. This victory destroyed the old KMT legal system and laid a solid foundation for the establishment of a people's democratic legal system. To help our readers better understand China's present socialist legal system, we will first outline the legal developments immediately preceding and following 1949.

When the Anti-Japanese War ended in 1945, the goal was to mobilize various democratic parties, and indeed the whole nation, to work for a people's democratic republic that would enforce revolutionary laws. The underlying idea was to improve

---

1 Compiled in 1740, *The Great Qing Dynasty Law* includes seven divisions such as law of usual practice, law of civil service, law of revenue, law of rites, law of war, law of justice and law of works, with four hundred and thirty-six articles. After the articles were ten hundred and forty-nine rules and regulations with the imperial memorials.

the legal system on the basis of democracy. Thus, on April 23, 1946, the CPC called the first session of the Third Counselors Conference of the Shaanxi—Gansu—Ningxia Border Area. [1] The conference adopted the Resolution of Constitutional Principles for the Shaanxi—Gansu—Ningxia Border Area, a charter for the entire border area. The resolution remained the most outstanding legislative document at the time of the People's War of Liberation.

The Constitutional Principles include five parts — organizations of political power, people's rights, the judiciary, economic policy, and cultural and educational policy:

Organizations of political power The Constitutional Principles state that "People's counselors conferences of the border area, counties, and townships are people's political administrative institutions." This sets forth people's political authorities at all levels. The counselors conferences at the time of the Anti-Japanese War were gradually evolving into a system of people's representative conferences. First, the people universally, directly, and equally cast secret ballots to elect representatives at different levels. Next, the people's representative conferences at various levels elected the respective people's government committees as administrative organizations.

People's rights The Constitutional Principles stipulate that the people enjoy full political freedom, and that the government should instruct and protect the people and help them materially. The people have the right to arm themselves. Besides enjoying the same rights as men do, women are to receive special attention from the government for their specific interests. In addition, all people are equal, regardless of nationality. National autonomous administrations can be organized in the communities of the minority nationalities. The minority nationalities may enact autonomous statutes as long as they do not conflict with the stipulations of the Constitutional Principles.

The judiciary The Constitutional Principles declare that "Judicial institutions at all levels exercise judicial power inde-

---

[1] It was the revolutionary base area set up by the CPC in the Second Revolutionary Civil War Period (1927–1937). After the Long March, in October 1935, it became the headquarters of the central CPC. The Shaanxi-Gansu-Ningxia Border Area Government was set up in September 1937.

11

pendently. They submit to law only, and are not subject to any interference." This establishes a vital judicial concept. The Constitutional Principles also provide that no organization or group shall make arrests or conduct interrogation, except for judicial and public security institutions which can exercise such power according to law. Judicial institutions are to pursue a policy of helping criminals change for better through education and persuasion.

Economic policy The Constitutional Principles specify that "The government should ensure land to the tillers, jobs to the laborers, and development opportunities to enterprises." Government institutions at all levels should strive to expand the economy and promote production.

Cultural and educational policy The Constitutional Principles stipulate that the government shall adopt effective measures to eliminate illiteracy, to develop cultural, educational, and health undertakings, to protect freedom of academic study, to promote scientific research, and to control diseases.

During this same period that the Constitutional Principles were adopted, the base areas led by the CPC enacted legislations governing land, civil, labor, and criminal affairs, and established a judicial system based on the people's democratic political power. People's judicial institutions were first established in large cities that had been liberated, where KMT judicial institutions had been destroyed. For example, on the eve of Beiping's (Beijing) liberation, a Judicial Organizations Takeover Group was organized within the city's Military Control Committee to promptly take over all KMT judicial organizations. The group suspended all KMT judicial personnel from office, disarmed them, and investigated and treated them individually according to each person's specific circumstances. Subsequently, the Beiping People's Court was founded in March 1949. The president of the People's Court headed a judicial committee, which led a civil affairs group and a criminal affairs group to make and enforce court decisions respectively.

At this time in early 1949, the judicial system continued to use effective methods adopted by the old liberated areas. However, as the number of new liberated areas grew and the people's democratic judicial institutions increased, new developments in the judicial system emerged:

A system of summons, search, and arrest was established. Any investigations by public security or judicial institutions had to be conducted strictly according to established legal procedure. Except for public security and judicial institutions, all organizations, groups, schools, factories, and shops were forbidden to search, arrest, detain, try, or punish any persons; offenders would be penalized for infringing personal rights.

Corporal punishment, including beating and unlawful killing, was banned. Citizens' security and health were protected and their personal rights safeguarded.

Legal proceedings were made free of charge. The people's courts were to firmly oppose bureaucratic ways, to handle cases for the sake of the people and their convenience, and to relieve the people's financial burden.

Simple and convenient methods of trials following the mass line were practiced. Rigid and over-elaborate methods that wasted manpower, material, or money were abandoned.

An appeal system was established. If a litigant pled not guilty and lost his or her case, he or she could, within a fixed period of time, appeal to a superior court. The superior court would hear the case again according to the procedure of intermediate appeal [1] to verify facts and arrive at a verdict.

A verification system was instituted in all liberated areas to help superior government and judicial institutions check and supervise the work of subordinate judicial institutions. Cases were reviewed. If a superior government or judicial institution discovered an erroneous verdict made by a subordinate judicial institution, it re-examined the case according to judicial verification procedures.

While the embryonic form of the people's judicial system was taking shape, the CPC Central Committee, in February 1949, published Instructions for Abolishing KMT's *Book of Six Laws* [2] and Determining Judicial Principles for Liberated

---

[1] Intermediate or first appeal is generally called trial of the second instance. While the trial level in China is called trial of the first instance.

[2] *Book of Six Laws* is a collection of major laws and regulations by the KMT, which includes the Constitution, civil law, commercial law, criminal law, civil procedure law and criminal procedure law and various related provisions.

Areas. In April, the North China People's Government promulgated the Directive of Abolishing the KMT *Book of Six Laws* and All Other Reactionary Laws. These were aimed at demolishing the KMT legal system and establishing the following principles:

Judicial institutions shall not refer to articles of the old laws for confirming verdicts.

People's judicial work in the liberated areas must be done according to new laws of the people's government. Before new laws are systematically enacted and promulgated, the people's courts should refer to CPC policies and other programs, laws, regulations, and resolutions published by the people's government and the People's Liberation Army (PLA).

Judicial departments must educate and remold the judicial personnel who were formerly under KMT rule according to individual circumstances. This will help revolutionize these judicial workers.

After the instructions were published, people's judicial institutions at all levels studied them conscientiously. The instructions helped clear up vague ideas and point out the directions in which work was needed. The ranks of the judiciary were consolidated, laying a solid foundation for methodically building up a people's democratic judicial system after the liberation of all of China.

FOUNDING AND DEVELOPMENT
OF THE PEOPLE'S DEMOCRATIC LEGAL SYSTEM

Representatives from the People's Democratic United Front organized the Chinese People's Political Consultative Conference (CPPCC) in the summer of 1949. By fall, the revolutionary forces had liberated the entire mainland except Guangzhou. It was time for the Chinese to unite and found a people's democratic state. According to a resolution of the CPPCC, the People's Republic of China was officially founded on October 1, 1949. A democratic legal system was established simultaneously.

The period from 1949 to 1953 was one of initiation for the

democratic legal system. During this period, the CPPCC was temporarily assuming the functions and powers of the National People's Congress, playing the role of the constitutional conference for the newborn People's Republic. The CPPCC adopted the Common Program of the Chinese People's Political Consultative Conference, [1] the Organic Law of the CPPCC, the Organic Law of the Central People's Government, and various resolutions regarding the national flag, the national anthem, and a new calendar. These documents acted as a provisional Constitution, opening a new era for building the legal system in China.

The Organic Law of the Central People's Government legally conferred on the Central People's Government Committee the status of being the highest institution of state power in China: The committee was to represent the People's Republic of China in foreign affairs and exercise state legislative power according to law. Thus, the Central People's Government Committee, adopting and promulgating many laws and decrees, was vital in nurturing the legal system. For example, the Marriage Law and the Land Law published in 1950 were the first important civil laws enacted by New China. The Regulations for Punishing Counterrevolutionaries and Regulations for Punishing Corruption, issued in 1951, were New China's earliest criminal laws. The Government Administrative Council of the Central People's Government also promulgated various administrative statutes.

Altogether, more than five hundred laws and ordinances were enacted during this initiation stage. Meanwhile, judicial institutions were established and improved, ensuring the enforcement and universal observance of law.

Between 1954 and 1957, the Chinese Government upheld the policy of governing the country according to law and took measures to strengthen democracy and the legal system. For instance, the First Session of the First National People's Congress was held in September 1954. Here, the NPC drafted and adopted the first Constitution of the People's Republic of China. Besides announcing that the NPC is the most fundamental part of the

---

[1] The Common Program made in September 1949 served as the provisional Constitution before the promulgation of the Constitution of the People's Republic of China in 1954.

political system of China, the Constitution brings the basic aspects of China's social system within the realm of law, providing legal grounds for practicing democracy and enforcing laws in China.

Another sign of the development of the legal system was the extensive enactment of laws and ordinances, which was essential for securing the nationwide enforcement of the Constitution, for strengthening the national economy, for maintaining public order and for guaranteeing citizens all kinds of democratic political rights including personal freedom and property rights. The Organic Law of the State Council, Organic Law of the People's Procuratorates, and Regulations for Arrest and Detention, promulgated in 1954, specified the functions, powers, and procedures of state administrative institutions, procuratorates, and public security departments. In a little over three years, more than five hundred laws and ordinances were adopted. This was a period during which New China's legal system developed most rapidly before the "cultural revolution."

Over the twenty years from the Anti-Rightist Movement in 1957 until the downfall of the Lin Biao and Jiang Qing's counterrevolutionary cliques in 1976, China's legal system nearly came to a standstill. On the heels of the Anti-Rightist Movement were the Great Leap Forward Campaign in 1958, the Four Clean-ups Movement 1963. [1] As a result of the frequent political movements, the "Left" political line had substantial influence in various areas, and legal nihilism was in vogue. This seriously interfered with the developing legal system: Over the twenty-year period from 1957 to 1976, altogether only less than four hundred laws and administrative statutes were published by the National People's Congress and the State Council. Even worse, violating the law became a common practice.

The "cultural revolution" started in 1966, when Red Guard

---

[1] The Four Clean-ups Movement, also called the Socialist Education Movement was a movement intended to clean up work-points, accounts, finances, and storehouses in villages, and politics, organizations, ideology, and finances in cities. It lasted from the winter of 1963 to the spring of 1966. It covered about one-third of the total counties and a few cities in the country. Though the movement had some good effects in correcting some unhealthy tendencies among the cadres and in economic management, it offered certain erroneous theories for the "cultural revolution."

organizations—army combat groups, rebel squads, and fighting brigades—mushroomed all over China. They seized and stole arms and ammunition by illegal means and built up armed organizations equipped with sticks, clubs, swords, rifles, cannons, and even warships. Bloody conflicts flared up between various factions and groups. China's legal system, which had begun to take shape, now fell apart. State legislative and judicial institutions were all placed under military control; normal legislative and judicial activities were suspended. It was a period of chaos when law was not observed. From this hard lesson, the Chinese people learned that if they want to ensure the stability and development of their state, and achieve democracy and modernization, they must eliminate pernicious vestiges of the feudal idea of "sovereign rules," and strictly enforce laws.

PERIOD OF RESTORATION AND DEVELOPMENT

In October 1976, reactionary coup d'etat of the two cliques headed by Lin Biao and Jiang Qing was smashed, ending the period of disorder and disruption. The CPC promptly led the people in correcting the errors of the "cultural revolution," bringing order out of chaos and setting wrongs right. It eradicated legal nihilism and the feudal notion of "sovereign rules," and adopted measures to strengthen socialist democracy and the law. China's legal system once again embarked on the path of normal development.

Since 1978, when the Third Plenary Session of the Eleventh CPC Central Committee and the Twelfth National People's Congress were held, China has achieved notable success in developing socialist democracy and the socialist legal system. The Third Session mapped out a set of guidelines for building democracy and the legal system. Its communique declares,

As China has not really practiced democratic centralism but has stressed centralism at the expense of democracy and enjoyed too little democracy in the past period, it is particularly necessary to strengthen democracy in the present period.... To safeguard people's democracy, we must strengthen the socialist legal system and systematize and legalize democracy, so that this system and its legality remain stable, lasting, and authoritative, to the extent that there are laws to refer to.... [The laws] must be strictly enforced, and any violations must be punished.

This spirit has prevailed. Indeed, China's post-1949 history has not seen such a heyday as now exists in democracy and the legal system. China's leaders have stated and reiterated that if China wants to achieve the four modernizations, [1] it must pay close attention at the same time to both the economy and the legal system. The leaders maintain that without a high level of democracy and a sound legal system, society would be unstable and it would be impossible to attain the four modernizations. Thus, due to and since the Third Plenary Session, the following results have been achieved:

Breaking into the restricted ideological areas and emancipating the mind This was a prerequisite to the restoration and development of China's legal system. In the past, people suffered mental stagnation, bound by feudal ideas. Such was particularly true in the legal arena, which was known as the "disastrously restricted area." People dared not give views on strengthening the legal system. Nor would they probe into specific legal problems. To institute true democracy and legality in China, therefore, it was necessary to first make a breakthrough in the ideological realm, to overcome the influence of various feudalistic ideas. It was necessary to imbue the masses with legal ideas and demonstrate the need for strengthening democracy and legality.

Accordingly, the Third Session called on the people to emancipate their minds and seek truth from facts. The Chinese people began to shake off a mental yoke and create a lively climate of democracy and freedom in ideological and theoretical areas. Jurists and legal workers now dared to combine the Chinese science of law with specific legislative and judicial prac-

---

[1] The four modernizations are goals of China's socialist construction. They are: modernization of industry; of agriculture; of science and technology; and of national defense.

18

tices and to draw on the experience of other countries. They held extensive and profound discussions on how to build a democratic legal system with Chinese characteristics. This served as a strong impetus to the development of democracy and legality in China.

Redressing wrong and mishandled cases To strengthen the legal system, China had to redress wrong cases that had been judged without observing the law; the legitimate rights and interests of the innocent people had to be defended. In 1979 people's courts at all levels began to review the cases tried during the " cultural revolution." Pursuing a policy of righting all wrongs, the courts, by the end of 1981, had redressed a total of 301,000 mishandled cases involving 326,000 persons. Many of the wronged persons were rehabilitated and appropriately compensated for. Next, cases handled during other political movements before the "cultural revolution" were re-examined and all wronged persons rehabilitated. Hundreds of thousands of innocent people who had been wrongly labeled as "Rightists" during the 1957 Anti-Rightist Movement were promptly exonerated. [1]

The redressing of wrongs not only assuaged the national trauma of the "cultural revolution" and promoted stability and unity, it also contributed to eradicating influences of feudalism and legal nihilism, establishing the authority of socialist democracy and legality, and increasing the cadres' sense of executing law and the citizens' sense of observing the law.

Revising the Constitution and improving the leadership and the political system of the state To reform and perfect state leadership and political system and promote legality, the Fifth NPC held its Third Session in 1980 and accepted the proposal of the CPC Central Committee that the Constitution [2] be revised. More than two years were then spent on discussing and revising

---

[1] See *Law Year Book of China*, China Law Press, 1987, p. 9.

[2] The first Constitution was made in the First Session of the First National People's Congress on September 20, 1954. The Constitution was revised on January 17, 1975, and again on March 5, 1978. And on December 4, 1982 the Fifth Session of the Fifth National People's Congress passed the new Constitution of the People's Republic of China which is still in effect. Important revisions of the 1982 Constitution concerning private economy and land were made in the First Session of the Seventh National People's Congress in April 1988.

articles of the Constitution. The new Constitution was officially adopted on December 4, 1982 and promulgated for enforcement.

Summing up positive and negative experiences in the years since the founding of the People's Republic, the new Constitution embraces a series of stipulations for improving state leadership and political system so as to consolidate socialist democracy and legality. This is shown by the following rules and principles:

Expanding the functions and powers of the NPC Standing Committee and raising its efficiency through specialization. The NPC has established six special committees under the Standing Committee — Nationalities Committee, Law Committee, Finance and Economy Committee, Education, Science, Culture, and Public Health Committee, Foreign Affairs Committee, and Overseas Chinese Committee. They are to study, consider, and draw up motions. (See the Constitution, Article 70)

Restoring the post of president of the state. The president represents the People's Republic of China in foreign affairs and domestic matters. (*Ibid.,* Article 81)

Establishing the Central Military Commission as an independent state institution to direct the armed forces of the country. The commission is headed by a chairman, who is responsible to the NPC and its Standing Committee. (*Ibid.,* Articles 93 and 94)

The premier has overall responsibility for the State Council. The ministers have overall responsibility for the ministries or commissions under their charge. (*Ibid.,* Article 86)

Strengthening the development of the local institutions of state power under the unified leadership of the central authorities, and enlarging the power of local state institutions. The local people's congresses at and above the county level are to establish their own standing committees. (*Ibid.,* Article 96)

Perfecting the system of autonomy in regions inhabited by minority nationalities, stepping up the development of these regions, and strengthening unity and mutual assistance among all nationalities. (*Ibid.,* Articles 112–122)

Reforming the rural commune system by integrating government administration with economic management, establishing government institutions at the township level, and strengthening the functions and development of grassroots state institutions. (*Ibid.*, Article 95)

Extending the people's democratic system at the grassroots level. People's deputies at and below the county level are directly elected by voters. Neighborhood residents' committees and villagers' committees serve as mass organizations of self-management at the grassroots level. (*Ibid.*, Article 97)

Abolishing the practice of life tenure of leading cadres. The president and vice-president of the state, the chairman and vice-chairmen of the NPC Standing Committee, and the premier and vice-premiers of the State Council shall serve no more than two consecutive terms, each term being five years. (*Ibid.*, Article 111)

Improving the legislative system and strengthening legislative work The greatest hindrance to legislative work in the past was the failure to specify the legislative power of the NPC and its Standing Committee. The new Constitution expands the functions and powers of the NPC Standing Committee to ensure normal legislative activities. It also specifies that no one on the Standing Committee shall hold any post in any administrative, judicial, or procuratorial institution of the state. This enables members of the Standing Committee to direct their time and energy to legislative duties and to specialize in their work. (*Ibid.*, Article 66)

When the NPC instituted the Law Committee in 1979, the Commission of Legislative Affairs was established to assist the Law Committee in legislative work. The Law Committee advised the NPC and its Standing Committee on means of developing democracy and strengthening the legal system. In turn, the NPC and its Standing Committee, over the past eight years (1979–1987), revised, supplemented, adopted, and ratified 121 laws, regulations, decisions, and resolutions. This included 61 laws, 60 decisions and resolutions on revising and supplementing laws. Meanwhile the State Council enacted over 500 administrative statutes, and people's congresses of provinces, municipalities, and autonomous regions and their standing committees promulgated about 900 local statutes.

All these laws and statutes, together with the new Constitution, have helped form a socialist legal system with Chinese characteristics.

Today, besides the Constitution, the state's fundamental law, China has Criminal Law, Criminal Procedure Law, Civil Procedure Law, and a number of other laws governing state institutions. Although there is still no unified civil code, there are separate laws that actually comprise parts of a civil code, such as the Marriage Law, Economic Contract Law, Patent Law, Trademark Law, and Inheritance Law. The Fourth Session of the Sixth NPC, held on March 25, 1986, adopted and promulgated China's first fundamental body of laws governing civil affairs — the General Rules of Civil Law — which marks the increasing perfection of China's civil legislation.

In addition, legislation in the economic arena has developed rapidly, as China emphasizes reform of the country's economic structure and pursues policies of invigorating the domestic economy and opening to the outside world. Since 1979, the NPC and its Standing Committee have enacted twenty-three economic laws and the State Council has promulgated and ratified sixty-two economic statutes.

Restoring the procuratorial system All Chinese procuratorial institutions were attacked and dismantled during the "cultural revolution." The 1975 Constitution retained procuratorial institutions in name, but turned their functions and powers over to public security institutions. Thus, both investigation and procuratorial powers were concentrated in the public security institutions. In 1978 China reorganized procuratorial institutions to ensure the correct enforcement of laws. Today, through the prosecution of crimes and violations of economic laws, the people's procuratorial institutions maintain public order according to law.

Restoring judicial administrative institutions To strengthen judicial administration, to successfully reform criminals and juvenile delinquents through labor, to publicize laws, and to secure the work of lawyers and notaries, the Eleventh Session of the Fifth NPC, in 1979, called for the restoration of the Ministry of Justice and its local judicial institutions. The judicial administrative system was quickly rebuilt throughout China.

Restoring the role of lawyers China had a number of practicing lawyers from March 1954 until June 1957. These lawyers, however, were repudiated during the Anti-Rightist Movement, and subsequently suffered a lengthy period of injustice and persecution. Not until after 1980 was the role of lawyers restored to attend to the fast-developing legal system. By the end of 1983, China had established two thousand legal consultation offices and lawyer offices encompassing fourteen thousand full- and part-time lawyers (fifty-five hundred full-time lawyers). The lawyers are now rendering a growing number of services to the people, e.g., providing representation in criminal and civil lawsuits and arbitration procedure. In addition, many lawyers have been appointed as permanent legal advisers to businesses and institutions, helping them apply the law to manage economic activities, to solve economic disputes, and to draft and negotiate contracts.

Restoring and improving the legal supervision system However perfect a law is, it still needs a supervision system to guarantee strict observance of the law by state institutions and citizens, and to prevent the law's administrators from violating or failing to execute the law. There is a well-known ancient Chinese legal saying: "Law won't work by itself." After 1978, China began to improve its legal supervision system. The result today is a two-pronged system. On the one hand, procuratorates oversee investigations by public security institutions and trials by people's courts. On the other hand, the NPC and its Standing Committee, and local people's congresses and their standing committees, the people's governments, people's courts, and people's procuratorates at the respective levels to ferret out unlawful acts and promptly correct them according to law.

Restoring and developing institutions of political science and law During the "cultural revolution," the vast majority of institutions and schools of political science and law were shut down, suspending nearly all of China's legal education. This left a void. After the downfall of the Gang of Four in 1976, China re-established political science and law schools and institutions around the country to raise the professional qualifications of judicial cadres and to develop nation-wide political and legal education. Today almost all provinces, municipalities and autonomous regions have their own political science and law institutions. Within the past few years, more than 160,000 cadres have been trained in such institutions and schools. Among them, 120,000 have graduated from institutions of higher learning. Part-time legal education has also developed. Over the last three years, China's correspondence law universities, law colleges on television, law colleges for self-study students, and evening law colleges have enrolled a total of 100,000 students.

Popularizing legal education The Chinese Government has popularized legal education in recent years. Adopting various methods and measures, it has helped citizens grasp the essence of state laws, increasing the nation's consciousness of law. In 1985, the NPC Standing Committee adopted the Resolution on Popularizing Legal Knowledge Among Citizens, calling on all state institutions, educational departments, and the mass media to publicize basic legal information about civil and criminal affairs and about state institutions. Today legal education is taught at 492 universities in China (thirty percent of the total number of universities) and in 87,000 high schools (ninety percent of the total).

China's democracy and legal system have begun to take shape with bright prospects. Although the building of a thorough democracy and a " perfect" legal system calls for further concerted efforts of the entire nation, China has already laid a reliable foundation for this cause.

First, China has pursued a correct orientation for development of the legal system. As China's socialist system improves, the legal system will make greater progress.

Second, the Chinese people have learned a profound lesson from the ten-year disorder. They recognize the need for strict enforcement of socialist democracy and laws. This recognition provides a real basis and impetus to the building of the legal system.

Third, modern socialist construction depends upon a strong socialist legal system. Without a high level of democracy and a sound legal system, it is impossible to achieve socialist modernization. As long as the Chinese Government works toward the four modernizations, the Chinese people have to work on building democracy and the legal system.

It is not easy to establish true democracy and a "perfect" legal system. History shows that capitalist democracy and legal systems have been gradually improved by the efforts of many generations. Likewise, the development and improvement of socialist democracy and legality will take a considerably long period. One must bear in mind that feudalism lasted several thousand years in Chinese history. Many people today have only a faint concept of democracy and legality. In addition, China is a developing Third World country, whose economy and culture are quite backward. We would expect that China's building of its legal system would meet with various difficulties and obstacles. Nevertheless, the decision to intensify the development of the legal system has been made, and will not be reversed. If the Chinese people, the legislative institutions, and the judicial institutions play their parts fully, the socialist China with a high level of democracy and a "perfect" legal system will emerge.

CHAPTER 2

Legislative System and Institutions

True democracy for China can exist only within the context of an effective legal framework which systematizes the democratic process. Consequently, the passage of laws by legislative bodies is presently the condition for perfecting China's socialist legal system. To systematize legislative work in a scientific way and increase the effectiveness of law-making nationwide, it is necessary to establish a legislative system.

LEGISLATIVE POWER AND AUTHORITY FOR ESTABLISHING RULES AND REGULATIONS

China's legal system consists of two major parts—laws and rules and regulations. Both are coercive measures of the state. Nevertheless, they are different in nature and level, and in their scope of application.

Laws mean the Constitution and basic statutes involving state institutions, criminal and civil affairs, as well as other laws enacted by the NPC Standing Committee. Rules and regulations mean administrative rules and regulations established or approved by the State Council, as well as local and autonomous ordinances formulated by local (autonomous regional, provincial and municipal) people's congresses and their standing committees.

The make-up of the Chinese legal system is illustrated in the following diagram:

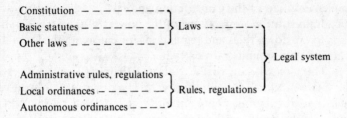

Laws define the standard of conduct in basic social life and are upheld throughout China. Rules and regulations, unlike laws, prescribe behavior in particular aspects of life; they take legal effect only in this realm. They shall not contravene laws, otherwise they are legally invalid.

Rules and regulations are generally derived from the Constitution and basic statutes enacted by the NPC as well as from other laws formulated by the NPC Standing Committee. The Constitution and laws are the source of various rules and regulations. Therefore, two kinds of law-making power have taken shape in China: legislative authority for enacting the Constitution, basic statutes and other laws; and authority for laying down administrative rules and regulations, local and autonomous ordinances.

Only state legislative institutions enjoy legislative power and exercise it. The NPC and its Standing Committee are vested by law with the legislative power of enacting the Constitution, basic statutes and other laws.

Rules and regulations include administrative, economic, local, and autonomous rules and regulations established on the basis of the Constitution, basic statutes and other laws, or according to the authorization of institutions of state power.

Article 85 of the Constitution says, "The State Council, that is, the Central People's Government of the People's Republic of China, is the executive body of the highest level of state power; it is the highest institution of state administration." The Constitution empowers the State Council to formulate administrative rules and regulations. These are standard measures for enforcing the Constitution, basic statutes, and other laws. They ensure the

27

implementation of the Constitution and laws, and their successful administration. In fact, one of the powers of the State Council is to lay down rules and regulations for enforcing the law and running state administrative affairs.

The Constitution or the National People's Congress vests the State Council with authority to lay down administrative rules and regulations. This authority is restricted by the NPC and must be based on the Constitution and on laws enacted by the NPC. The NPC has the right to abolish administrative rules and regulations of the State Council that contradict the Constitution and various other laws. If local rules and regulations or autonomous ordinances conflict with the State Council's administrative rules and regulations, they would be abolished by the NPC Standing Committee, not by the State Council.

Provincial people's congresses and their standing committees, as China's local institutions of state power, establish local rules and regulations. This power, however, is restricted not only by the Constitution, basic statutes and other laws, but also by administrative rules and regulations formulated by the State Council, and therefore, must not be contravened. Although they are not administrative or judicial institutions, the provincial people's congresses have the duty to "ensure the observance and implementation of the Constitution, the statutes and the administrative rules and regulations in their respective administrative areas." (Article 99 of the Constitution) Therefore, the local ordinances they pass are detailed rules and regulations for enforcing the laws and administrative rules in different localities. These ordinances, therefore, ensure the implementation of the Constitution, statutes, and administrative rules and regulations.

The people's congresses of national autonomous regions have the power to enact autonomous ordinances and separate regulations according to the political, economic and cultural characteristics of the local nationalities. This power is vested by the Constitution or the highest level of state power on the basis of the principle of regional national autonomy. But these autonomous ordinances and regulations must be reported to the NPC Standing Committee for approval before they can come into force. Autonomous ordinances and separate regulations enacted by the people's congresses of prefectures and counties must be reported to the people's congresses and standing committees of respective provinces or autonomous regions for approval and to the NPC Standing Committee for the record before they can come into force. This ensures that the NPC Standing Committee has the final power of confirming autonomous ordinances and regulations.

Back in 1954, China's first Constitution stipulated that national autonomous regions had the power to enact autonomous ordinances and separate regulations. It defined the NPC as the only legislative institution. In his article *On the Ten Major Relationships*, Mao Zedong said,

> According to our Constitution, the legislative powers are all vested in the central authorities. But, provided that the policies of the central authorities are not violated, the local authorities may work out rules, regulations and measures in the light of their specific conditions and the needs of their work, and this is in no way prohibited by the Constitution.

The power of enacting local and autonomous ordinances by local and regional national autonomous institutions of state power is not part of the legislative power defined by the Constitution, but rather a power of passing rules and regulations.

Unlike pure legislative power, the power of passing administrative, local and autonomous rules and regulations comes from the highest level of state power and is under its supervision. The initiating power (the source of power) and final supervisory power (the power of abolition) of any legally effective standard documents in China, including administrative, local and autonomous rules and regulations, come from the NPC and its Standing Committee, which are vested with legislative power. This shows that China's legislative system is jointly composed of its legislative institution— the NPC and its Standing Committee — the highest level of state power, and the State Council— the highest state administrative apparatus. In addition, there are provincial conduits of state power leading from the State Council to the provincial people's congresses and their standing committees. These institutions enjoy the power of formulating rules and regulations.

ESTABLISHMENT OF
LEGISLATIVE INSTITUTIONS

Unlike most Western countries, China does not have a state system that separates legislative, executive, and judicial functions. Instead, it builds one on the basis of the National People's Congress by combining the functions of parliament and government.

China's NPC system is a unified legislative system which concentrates legislative power within the central authorities and has the absolute power of enacting laws. There is only one legislative source in the Chinese Government, and only one legislative and legal system. Although the highest state administrative institution and local institutions of state power are authorized by the NPC to draw up legally effective "standard documents," these "documents" are subordinate to the Constitution and laws enacted by the NPC. The highest level of state administration and other sources of state power are not entitled to independent and complete legislative power. The legally valid documents they produce are parts of the unified legal system and do not form a parallel and independent legal system.

The NPC and its Standing Committee exercise state legislative power and enact the Constitution, basic statutes and other laws. Meanwhile, the State Council and the provincial people's congresses and their standing committees have the power to lay down administrative, local, and autonomous rules and regulations. With such concentration and unity of legislative power, China has developed a legislative system with uniquely Chinese characteristics to suit the specific conditions of China with its vast area, abundant resources and huge population. This is a **unified** legislative system with **two orders** and **three divisions**.

Unification means that the NPC and its Standing Committee exercise state legislative power in a unified manner. Only they have the right to enact and revise basic statutes and other laws. They form the source of power for other state institutions to draw up standard documents that have legal force. The Constitution and laws they enact are the legal source from which other legally valid documents arise. The Constitution, statutes and laws, as well as the administrative, local and autonomous rules and regulations deriving from them, make up China's unified legal system.

The **two orders**—the NPC and its Standing Committee—form the highest level of state power and exercise in unison state legislative power. They are different from the two-chambered system of many countries. One is not necessarily superior or inferior and there is no connotation of subordination. They are, in fact, two different orders complementing each other. They comprise a division of labor in legislative power and each enjoys appropriate independent legislative power. Working separately, they enact and amend the Constitution, basic statutes, and other laws. Although there is some difference in authority and legal force between the two, all laws and legal documents adopted by the NPC Standing Committee can be directly promulgated for implementation by the president of the state and require no approval of the NPC.

Nevertheless, the NPC could alter or revoke any improper resolutions of its Standing Committee (improper laws included). The latter, however, has the right to interpret the Constitution and to propose amendments to it, supplementing the NPC power of enacting the Constitution. It can also make amendments to basic statutes enacted by the NPC on condition that this does not contradict the basic principle of the statutes. This right of interpretation, revision, and amendment is an effective and timely feedback regulation for the Constitution and basic statutes adopted by the NPC.

The concept of a unified legislative system and its two orders extends the legislative power of the NPC to its Standing Committee, so as to increase the efficiency of state legislation as a whole. In addition, it sets a precedent for the Standing Committee of a unitary socialist source of state power to exercise legislative power.

The **three divisions** mean that the NPC, through the Constitution, authorizes the State Council to lay down administrative rules and regulations, vests the power of enacting local ordinances in the people's congresses and their standing committees of provinces, municipalities and autonomous regions, and empowers national autonomous regions to establish autonomous ordinances. These are the three kinds of power of formulating rules and regulations deriving from the legislative power of the NPC. They are also the three branches subordinate to the legislative power of the NPC and its Standing Committee, and the three kinds of rules and regulations subordinate to the Constitution and statutes.

The three divisions are related to the NPC and its Standing Committee by way of legal supervision with each division having a different relationship to the NPC. The three divisions, therefore, assume a different legal status and take on separate tasks in China's legislative system.

China's unified legislative system with two orders and three divisions is illustrated on the following page.

This diagram shows a comprehensive legislative system with Chinese characteristics. All essential elements in this system form an organic whole. The NPC and its Standing Committee are the control center of the entire legislative system, the source of power for all other state institutions. They are related to the three divisions according to established orders and specific methods, each fulfilling its own function. All the essential elements of this legislative system connect with and act on each other to form a unified whole, involving the central and local authorities, institutions of power and executive, legislative and administrative bodies. They carry out a complete regulation of Chinese society.

The locus of power in the legislative system—the NPC and its Standing Committee— connects with the three divisions indirectly by power vested through the Constitution and legal supervision, not directly through administrative leadership. Because the three divisions—the State Council, the provincial people's congresses and their standing committees, and the regional autonomous people's congresses and their standing committees—each have different limits on their vested power, they differ from each other in their relationships to the NPC and its Standing Committee. This will be dealt with separately in other chapters.

DIAGRAM OF CHINA'S LEGISLATIVE SYSTEM

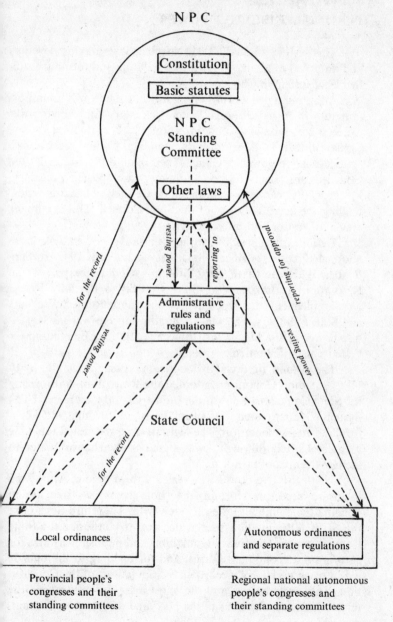

SYSTEM OF
VESTING LEGISLATIVE POWER

This system gradually takes shape as law-making develops and improves in China. It is vital to building and forming a unified legal system in China.

Adopting a process of vesting legislative power is an important reform in a legislative system necessary for carrying out China's economic modernization. According to the Constitution, the NPC and its Standing Committee exercise state legislative power in China. Their main duty is to enact the Constitution, basic statutes and other laws. When necessary, however, they can authorize the State Council to enact laws, extending the legal authority of the State Council. This is China's system of vesting legislative power.

Definite measures of vesting legislative power have been adopted three times since China was liberated in 1949. In September 1983, the Sixth NPC Standing Committee passed the Resolution Authorizing the State Council to Partially Revise and Supplement the Document Concerning Retired Workers and Staff Members. This was the first instance of vesting legislative power in the history of Chinese legislation. But the power vested was quite limited.

The second time was in September 1984, when the Sixth NPC Standing Committee adopted the Resolution Authorizing the State Council to Reform the Industrial and Commercial Tax System, Draft Related Tax Regulations, and Promulgate Them for Trial Implementation. The legislative power vested this time was also limited although it was already somewhat expanded to include the area of taxation.

The legislative power was vested a third time in April 1985 to ensure success in reforming the whole economic system and in opening the country to the outside world. The Third Session of the Sixth NPC made a special decision to authorize the State Council to pass temporary regulations and publish measures for carrying out economic reforms, and for opening to the outside world when necessary, according to stipulations of the Constitution. These regulations and measures must not contravene the related laws and decisions of the NPC and its Standing Committee, and the State Council should report them to the NPC Standing Committee for the record. After a trial period and when conditions are appropriate, the NPC or its Standing Committee would make them into laws.

In the past few years, the NPC has time and again vested legislative power in the State Council. This is indicative of the maturation of China's system of vesting legislative power which has the following characteristics:

First, the vesting of legislative power extends the legislative power of the State Council. Under the 1982 Constitution, the State Council has the right to lay down administrative rules and regulations according to the Constitution and laws. Some legislative power originally exercised by the NPC and its Standing Committee is now partially vested in the State Council on certain conditions allowing establishment of special administrative rules and regulations. In other words, the State Council now enjoys new legislative power for formulating and putting into effect temporary regulations.

Second, the legislative power vested in the State Council is especially defined in the resolution of authorization. For example, the latest authorization of legislative power clearly stipulates economic reforms and opening policy.

Third, after a period of trial and practice and when conditions are proper, the temporary regulations laid down by the State Council would be made into laws by the NPC or its Standing Committee. This shows that these regulations are different from ordinary administrative regulations already in legal force. We may say the highest institution of state power vests the State Council with the power of enacting "quasi-laws."

Fourth, the State Council is subject to the supervision of the NPC. The limits of vested legislative power are clearly defined in the authorizing resolution. Basically, the rules and regulations established by the State Council must not contravene the basic principles of the related laws and resolutions adopted by the NPC and its Standing Committee.

Finally, when the State Council formulates temporary rules or regulations, it must report them to the NPC Standing Committee for the record. Then, when conditions are appropriate, the NPC or its Standing Committee can make them into laws.

This shows that the authorization of legislative power is a temporary measure suitable to a particular stage.

Since the beginning of the 1980s, rapid development of China's system of vesting legislative power is inevitable. An important legal mechanism for a modern country to strengthen administration, this system of vesting legislative power also promotes development of the state, a reflection of the positive consequences of the re-establishment of China's legal system and the restructuring of its economy.

China's nationwide economic reforms centering on cities while opening to the outside world involve methodical work done according to correct principles. To carry out its reforms properly, China must establish a legal system with the ability to handle effectively any new problems. Rules and regulations should be turned promptly into laws. The State Council should effectively pass necessary administrative rules and regulations. Nevertheless, there are many complicated new problems that go beyond the scope of administrative rules and regulations and the necessary practical experience for solving them. This situation calls for careful experimentation, exploration and reasonable improvisation. The practical work cannot wait for the NPC or its Standing Committee to revise or pass supplemental laws. If problems are not quickly tackled, they could block economic reforms and undo the positive results of not only China's open door policy but the system of vesting legislative power.

The extension and application of this authorization of legislative power not only meets the urgent need for practical work, but also helps the NPC or its Standing Committee to enact, revise or supplement laws. This smooths the way for economic and administrative legislation. This system of vesting legislative power, therefore, is a *sine qua non* for China's state legislative system.

LEGISLATIVE PROCEDURE

China's laws define not only legislative power but also legislative procedure. Past legislative practices have formed a basis for modern legislative procedure with Chinese characteristics.

Today, many practices of legislative institutions are inter-connected. Therefore, different stages of legislative procedure are linked together. China's legislative procedure falls into the following four stages:

Submitting a draft of the law At this first stage of legislative procedure, the authorized institution and personnel submit a draft of the law to the legislative institution, which places the draft on its agenda as an item for discussion. It is the legislative source's duty to discuss the draft and make a decision adopting or rejecting it.

Drafts of laws must be proposed and submitted according to specific legal procedure to produce the corresponding legal effect. Only authorized institutions and personnel can submit formal drafts of laws. Those that are unauthorized can give their views and suggestions for legislation in various ways such as publishing articles in newspapers or journals, writing letters or making speeches. They can say what they think about enacting, revising, or abolishing certain laws. But because these methods are not within the formal legal procedural framework they have no legal force. Moreover, these views and suggestions are not to be placed on the agenda of the legislative institutions for discussion.

China's legislative institutions are made up of people's deputies. They should pay great attention to the voice and demands of the people and respect their collective will. The will of the people, however, is not the same as the wishes of individuals. Only by practicing a high degree of centralism on the basis of democracy can we reflect the true will of the people. This principle of democratic centralism is underlined by China's rule that only authorized institutions and personnel can submit drafts of laws according to legal procedure.

According to stipulations of the Constitution and the NPC Organic Law, it is possible for the NPC Presidium, the NPC Standing Committee, the NPC special committees, the State Council, the Central Military Commission, the Supreme People's Court and the Supreme People's Procuratorate to submit to the NPC motions that fall within the NPC's functions and powers. These institutions can all submit motions to the NPC Standing Committee that are within its functions and powers. At the same time, a quorum of thirty or more NPC deputies can submit motions to the NPC. In additions, a membership of ten or above of the NPC Standing Committee can submit motions to the NPC Standing Committee. All these stipulations define what institutions and members have the right to submit motions, and delineate their particular responsibilities for legislation.

Discussing the draft laws This means formal examination and argument made by the legislative institutions on drafts of laws that have been placed on the agenda. It includes discussion by citizens organized by the legislative institutions who air their specific views, which are then collected for consideration when the drafts of laws are formally discussed.

To carry out the mass line well in legislative work, China urges its citizens to open extensive discussion about drafts of laws. Law research institutes, law colleges, and law groups might hold symposiums and forums to propose specific amendments and addenda to drafts of laws. All this, however, is outside formal discussion within the legislative procedure.

According to stipulations of the Constitution, the various special committees established by the NPC are to study, examine, and work out respective motions under the guidance of the NPC and its Standing Committee. All drafts of laws shall be examined and discussed by the NPC Law Committee. Other special committees might propose to the Law Committee to make specific amendments and addenda to the drafts of respective laws. This system contributes to careful and meticulous discussion on drafts of laws, ensuring their quality.

The NPC arranges for examination and discussion about drafts of laws in the following way. First, NPC deputies organize delegations according to election units. Then each delegation elects a head and a deputy head. Before each NPC meeting is held, all delegations discuss the subjects prepared for the meeting by the NPC Standing Committee. In the course of the NPC session, they examine and discuss the drafts of laws and all other motions submitted to the NPC. The head of a delegation, or a representative elected by the delegation, might air views on the law drafts and motions at meetings of the NPC Presidium or at NPC sessions on behalf of the delegation. Before any draft of law or motion is put to vote at a NPC session, the maker of the motion can withdraw it, and discussion about it shall stop.

The discussion of drafts of laws by the NPC Standing Committee usually goes through two stages. At the first stage, the authorized institution or personnel would give an explanation on the law drafts to the NPC Standing Committee. The NPC Standing Committee discusses them and proposes some amendments. Then the NPC Law Committee and the Commission of Legislative Affairs of the NPC Standing Committee, or other authorized institutions, correct the drafts of laws according to the proposal of the NPC Standing Committee. At the second stage when the NPC Standing Committee meets again (once in two months), the NPC Law Committee or another authorized institution gives an explanation on the corrections to the meeting. After being discussed and amended once again, the drafts of laws are finally put to a vote. If the person who proposes of a draft law withdraws it before it is put to a vote at a meeting of the NPC Standing Committee, discussion on the draft stops.

Voting laws through This means the procedure for a legislative institution to vote on draft laws formally, turning them into laws. Therefore, this is a crucial stage in the whole legislative procedure.

According to Chinese laws, any draft of a law must be put to a vote after it has been examined and discussed. Any amendments to the Constitution must be proposed by the NPC Standing Committee or one-fifth or more members of the NPC. It must be passed by a two-thirds majority of the NPC membership. Laws and other motions must be adopted by half of the NPC membership. Law drafts and other motions discussed by the NPC Standing Committee shall be passed by half of its membership.

Implementing and enforcing laws The legislative institutions officially put into effect laws that have been adopted. When a law is being put into effect, it can be publicized by broadcasting and TV stations, newspapers, journals and books. But this does not come within the category of legislative procedure.

According to constitutional stipulations, the president of the state promulgates laws adopted by the NPC and its Standing Committee in accordance with their resolutions.

The promulgation of a law is closely related to its enforcement. Before its formal promulgation, no law can be regarded as having taken legal effect; that is, no law can be enforced. Nevertheless, the time of promulgation and the time of enforcement are not always the same.

There are three significant dates that mark the coming into force of laws after they are promulgated in China.

A law can become effective and be enforced on the date of promulgation, such as the Chinese-Foreign Joint Ventures Law which was adopted on July 1, 1979, and then promulgated and enforced on July 8.

Some laws can be enforced after a period of time following their promulgation, such as the Criminal Law, which was adopted on July 1, 1979 and promulgated on July 7, but was enforced nationwide later on January 1, 1980.

After their promulgation, some laws are enforced on different dates in different places, according to the time of arrival of the law in near and far-away areas. But this is increasingly becoming rare.

CHAPTER 3

Supreme Source of State Authority

The National People's Congress is China's supreme source of state authority while its Standing Committee is its permanent representative. According to Article 58 of the Constitution, the NPC and its Standing Committee exercise legislative power of the state. They may revise the Constitution and enact basic statutes and other laws.

HIGHEST SOURCE OF STATE POWER

The NPC is made up of deputies elected by China's provinces, autonomous regions, municipalities directly under the Central Government, and the military. Through the NPC deputies they have elected, the Chinese people collectively exercise supreme authority in administrating major state affairs.

NPC deputies come from all social strata and circles, a fact guaranteed by election procedure and regulations. They also enjoy high popularity. The NPC can ensure administration of basic state affairs according to the will of the Chinese people. There are a number of reasons for this:

The NPC has the broadest mass foundation It is made up entirely of people's deputies voted by general election across the country. All citizens of the People's Republic of China who have reached the age of eighteen have the right to vote and stand for election, regardless of nationality, race, sex, occupation, family background, religious belief, education, property status, or length of residence. Without strict legal procedure, no citizen shall be deprived of the right to vote and stand for election.

The NPC forms the largest body of political representation for the Chinese people It consists of nearly three thousand deputies of more than fifty nationalities coming from thirty provinces, autonomous regions and municipalities directly under the Central Government, and the military. Selected by nationwide election, these deputies include representatives of all nationalities, all democratic parties and people's organizations, and include workers, peasants, scientists, combat heroes, writers, artists and educators. With such extensive representation, the NPC fully executes the fundamental will of all the Chinese people, while taking into account the historical characteristics of different areas and nationalities, as well as the special interests and demands of different classes.

The NPC is subject to the supervision of all the people and is responsible to them The NPC deputies should always maintain close ties with the voters in various ways according to law. They should earnestly represent the people's will and interests and reflect their voices and demands. According to law, the voters have the right to supervise the activities of their deputies and to recall or replace them. This process ensures that the people's deputies will represent the people's interests and reflect their will and needs.

To guarantee the NPC correctly exercises the highest state power and makes decisions on major state issues, the Constitution stipulates that the NPC can establish a number of special committees. Today, the Nationalities Committee, Law Committee, Finance and Economic Committee, Education, Science, Culture and Public Health Committee, Foreign Affairs Committee, and Overseas Chinese Committee are all under the NPC.

The duties of the NPC special committees are to examine, discuss and propose related motions, to address inquiries, and to consider cases where the Constitution and laws have been violated. They also investigate major issues and make proposals. At the same time, the NPC can also organize an investigative committee to deal with a special issue.

The NPC special committees are led by the NPC and, when

the NPC is not in session, by the NPC Standing Committee. Each special committee is composed of a chairman, some vice-chairmen and a number of members. The chairman conducts the work and meetings of the special committee. He is assisted by the vice-chairmen. Each special committee can appoint a number of specialists as advisers depending on need. The advisers may attend meetings of the special committee and present their opinions.

The special committees help the NPC exercise its role as the supreme source of state power and bring into play its part in deciding major state affairs on behalf of the whole nation. According to the Constitution, the power of the NPC is shown in the following four aspects:

—The legislative power of making amendments to the Constitution, enacting and amending basic statutes concerning criminal offenses, civil affairs, the state institutions and other matters.

—The power of electing the president and vice-president of the People's Republic of China; of deciding on the choice of the premier of the State Council upon nomination by the president; of deciding on the choice of the vice-premiers, state councilors, ministers in charge of ministries or commissions, and the auditor-general and secretary-general of the State Council upon nomination by the premier; of electing the chairman of the Central Military Commission and, upon nomination by the chairman, deciding on the choice of all the others on the Central Military Commission; of electing the president of the Supreme People's Court and the procurator-general of the Supreme People's Procuratorate.

The NPC also has the right to recall or remove these personnel from office according to law.

—The power of supervising the enforcement of the Constitution and the work of the NPC Standing Committee. The NPC has the right to alter or annul inappropriate decisions of the NPC Standing Committee.

—The power of examining and approving the plan for national economic and social development and the report on its implementation; of examining and approving the state budget and the report on its implementation; of approving the establishment of provinces, autonomous regions, and municipalities directly under the Central Government; of deciding on the establishment of special administrative regions and the systems to be instituted there; and of deciding on questions of war and peace.

Apart from exercising powers of legislation, supervision, election, recall, examination and approval, the NPC wields other powers. It assumes the highest legal status in the political and economic life of the state. One of its most important functions is to exercise legislative power, and carry on legislative work.

LEGISLATIVE POWER OF THE NPC

Being the supreme source of state power in China, the NPC executes the highest authority in the name of the Chinese people. Therefore, it is entitled to supreme legislative power. In essence, it can enact any law. Nevertheless, to define the division of function between the NPC and its Standing Committee, the Constitution has, in principle, delineated the limits of the NPC's legislative power. Generally speaking, the NPC has the following legislative powers:

Amending the Constitution The Constitution is China's fundamental law. Providing the framework for legality, the Constitution defines the basic principles underlying China's state and social systems, such as the nature of the state, political, economic, and military systems, the relationships between nationalities, the state structure, and basic rights and duties of citizens. These principles form the legal framework for various activities of the state.

Being the supreme source of legality, the Constitution is vital to the state's political economy. Consequently, the procedure for enacting and amending the Constitution is different from that for other laws. It is necessary to establish a draft committee or an amendment committee to enact or amend the Constitution.

Only the NPC has the power to amend the Constitution. According to related laws, amendment to the Constitution are to be proposed by the NPC Standing Committee or by more than one-fifth of the deputies to the NPC and adopted by a majority vote of more than two-thirds of all the NPC deputies. After working out the draft of the Constitution or of the revised Constitution, the NPC must solicit opinions from all social circles and submit it to the whole people for discussion. Then the draft is corrected according to the views of the entire nation and finally discussed and adopted by the NPC.

Because the enactment and amendment of the Constitution involves a democratic process that voices the will and desires of the people, it reflects their fundamental interests and promotes socialism. The leadership of the CPC is essential to the enactment and amendment of the Constitution. The CPC should unite with all of the Chinese people, including all other democratic parties and people's organizations, to uphold the Constitution and ensure its enforcement.

Enacting and amending criminal and civil laws Criminal and civil laws form the most important part of the basic statutes of any country. Their substance and enforcement have a direct bearing on the nature of a state, and its rise and decline. They are vital for administering a country. Therefore, it is necessary to entrust the NPC with the power to enact and amend directly criminal and civil laws.

The laws of criminal affairs constitute criminal law and the criminal procedure law. The laws of civil affairs constitute civil law and the civil procedure law. From legal standards of procedure, civil and criminal laws define the basic principles in civil and criminal lawsuits, and ensure the effective enforcement of laws.

The civil and criminal laws concern various areas of social life and bear directly on the vital interests of each citizen. Indicative of China's dedication to serving the interests of its people is the entrusting to the NPC of the power of enactment and amendment of civil and criminal laws. By enactment and amendment of these laws, the NPC protects the people's democratic rights, their personal and property rights, the property rights of the state and the collective, and preserves order in work, production, education, scientific research and the safety of each citizen.

Enacting and amending the basic statutes of state structures State structures form the main bodies exercising the functions of the state. Through the specific activities of state structures, the government runs the state and handles state affairs. Basic statutes of state structures are organic laws which define legal status, organizational structure, term of office of cadres, state administrative institutions, judicial institutions and procuratorial institutions.

Enacting and amending other basic statutes These include Election Law, Nationality Law, Marriage Law, Chinese-Foreign Joint Ventures Law and Law Concerning Enterprises with Exclusive Foreign Investment. Each of these laws specifies the principle of action in a certain important aspect of social life. They harmonize some essential relationships in political and social life, and play an important part in ensuring normal order in the entire society. For example, the Marriage Law has a bearing on every citizen and family, and has a direct impact on personal happiness, family harmony, and social progress. The Law Concerning Enterprises with Exclusive Foreign Investment defines the legal status, civil rights and management of these businesses. It is a major law involving China's open policy. The enactment of these laws by the NPC show that the people are masters in their own house, and ensures the embodiment of the people's will.

NPC STANDING COMMITTEE

One of the prevalent characteristics of the NPC is that it practices full democracy and upholds the principle of democratic centralism. All powers of the NPC should be collectively exercised by the NPC. But the NPC meets only once a year. When it is not in session, it leaves many affairs to a permanent office. This office stems from the appointment of the NPC Standing Committee which, according to the Constitution, is a permanent institution of the NPC and an essential part of the highest source of state power in China.

The NPC Standing Committee is composed of a chairman, vice-chairmen, a secretary-general and a number of members. They are elected from the deputies by the NPC. No one on the NPC Standing Committee shall hold post in any of the administrative, judicial or procuratorial institutions of the state. The reason is to ensure that they can discharge their functions well.

The chairman of the NPC Standing Committee convenes meetings and conducts its work. He is assisted by the vice-chairmen and secretary-general. He could delegate a vice-chairman to perform part of his functions. When the chairman falls ill and is unable to work or attend meetings, the NPC Standing Committee elects someone on the committee as acting-chairman until the chairman recovers from his illness or the NPC elects a new chairman.

The chairman, vice-chairmen and secretary-general of the NPC Standing Committee come together in a chairmen's conference to handle day-to-day work. The NPC Standing Committee also establishes a Credentials Committee to check the qualifications of the deputies.

In addition, the NPC Standing Committee institutes a general office under the leadership of the secretary-general. When necessary, the NPC Standing Committee may establish a work committee as its working agency. At present there is one such committee—the Commission of Legislative Affairs. Not to be confused with the NPC Law Committee, the Commission of Legislative Affairs is not part of the institution of state power but is an office of the NPC Standing Committee. Its primary task is to make draft laws.

According to stipulations of the Constitution and NPC Organic Law, the NPC Standing Committee primarily exercises the following functions and powers:

Legislative power That involves the enactment and amendment of laws other than those enacted by the NPC. When the NPC is not in session, the NPC Standing Committee has the right to make non-principle partial amendment and addenda to laws enacted by the NPC, and to interpret the Constitution and laws.

Supervisory power That involves the enforcement of the Constitution to annul those administrative rules and regulations, decisions or orders of the State Council that contravene the Constitution or statutes. It can also annul those local regulations or decisions of the institutions of state power of provinces, autonomous regions and municipalities directly under the Central

47

Government that contravene the Constitution, statutes, or administrative rules and regulations. The NPC Standing Committee also supervises the work of the State Council, the Central Military Commission, the Supreme People's Court and the Supreme People's Procuratorate.

Decision-making power When the NPC is not in session, the NPC Standing Committee decides, upon nomination by the premier of the State Council, on the choice of ministers in charge of the ministries or commissions, the auditor-general, and secretary-general of the State Council. It also passes on the choice of members of the Central Military Commission upon nomination by the chairman of the commission; on the appointment and recall of plenipotentiary representatives abroad; on the ratification and abrogation of treaties and important agreements concluded with foreign countries; on conferring state medals and titles of honor; on instituting systems of titles and ranks for military and diplomatic personnel and of other specific titles and ranks; on the granting of special pardons; on the proclamation of war; on general or partial mobilization; on the enforcement of martial law throughout the country or in particular provinces, autonomous regions, or municipalities directly under the Central Government.

When the NPC is not in session, it has the power to examine and approve partial adjustments to the plan for national economic and social development and to the state budget when it proves to be necessary in the course of their implementation.

The power of appointing and removing high officials from office The NPC Standing Committee appoints and removes vice-presidents and judges of the Supreme People's Court, members of its Judicial Committee and the president of the Military Court at the suggestion of the president of the Supreme People's Court, and deputy procurators-general and procurators of the Supreme People's Procuratorate, members of its Procuratorial Committee and the chief procurator of the Military Procuratorate at the suggestion of the procurator-general of the Supreme People's Procuratorate; and approves the appointment and removal of the chief procurators of the people's procuratorates of provinces, autonomous regions and municipalities directly under the Central Government. It also exercises

48

other functions and powers that the NPC may assign.

According to law, the NPC Standing Committee, as the permanent agency of the highest source of state power, enjoys part of the functions and powers of the NPC, including the most important power of legislation.

LIMITS OF LEGISLATIVE POWER OF
THE NPC STANDING COMMITTEE

In legislative practice, the NPC Standing Committee generally meets once every two months, whereas the NPC meets once a year. Each of these meetings is to examine and pass legal motions. Therefore, the NPC Standing Committee handles a large amount of legislative work, and plays an essential part in China's legislative system. Nevertheless, the law sets limits to the legislative power of the NPC Standing Committee. Such limits are as follows:

— The NPC Standing Committee has the power to enact and amend laws other than those enacted by the NPC. The NPC exercises legislative power on only fundamental political and economic issues of the state. Many other laws must be enacted if China is to modernize systematically and legally management of its economic and social life to meet the new developments in international economic exchanges. For example, progress of the sciences and technology, and the development of production call for laws governing environmental protection and natural resource protection. The expansion of economic and trade relations call for laws governing trademarks, patents and safe shipping. The enactment of such laws involving specific aspects of social life also comes within the limits of legislative power of the NPC Standing Committee. Since the Second Session of the Fifth NPC, the legislative work of the NPC Standing Committee has attracted keen attention. A large amount of legislative work has been done by the NPC Standing Committee, which promulgated a number of laws, rules and regulations, resolutions and decisions. All this has greatly contributed to the building of China's legal system.

— When the NPC is not in session, the NPC Standing

Committee makes partial amendments and addenda to basic statutes enacted by the NPC. Laws that have already been enacted and promulgated should be promptly amended and supplemented when circumstances have undergone new developments and radical changes. This is an essential part of legislative work. Both social life and legislation call for such amendments and addenda. Nevertheless, the NPC meets only once a year and is frequently unable to promptly amend enacted laws to meet new developments. This task is necessarily taken up by its permanent institution—the Standing Committee. On March 8, 1982 the NPC Standing Committee amended the Criminal Law to cope with a growing number of serious cases of smuggling, illegal purchase and sale of foreign money, speculation, profiteering, stealing public property, reselling rare cultural relics, asking for or accepting bribes, and drug trafficking. The amendments increased the punishment for these crimes, playing an important part in stabilizing public order.

Then, in 1983 the NPC Standing Committee amended a number of basic statutes to perfect them, such as organic laws for the people's courts and people's procuratorates.

— To ensure the correct enforcement of laws nationwide, the government must increase the general understanding of the articles of laws. It is necessary to explain their specific meanings. Although theoretical explanation has some impact on legislative and judicial work, it has no binding legal force. Only an authoritative legislative or judicial interpretation can have legal effect. According to the stipulations of the Constitution, the NPC Standing Committee has the right to interpret the Constitution and laws. This legislative interpretation is universally binding on all state institutions and their personnel. This is vital to perfecting the entire legal system. On June 10, 1981 the NPC Standing Committee adopted the Resolution on Strengthening the Work of Interpreting Laws to improve democracy and legality.

— The Constitution vests the NPC Standing Committee with the legal power of supervision to ensure the unification of the legal system. The NPC Standing Committee has the right to annul administrative rules, regulations, and orders established by the State Council that contravene the Constitution and its laws, as well as local rules, regulations and resolutions formulated by institutions of state power within the provinces, autonomous regions and municipalities directly under the Central Government that contravene the Constitution and laws. This is an essential part of legislative power, an indispensable measure for ensuring the unification and integrity of the state legal system.

CHAPTER 4

The State Council and Administrative Rules and Regulations

Administrative rules and regulations are the general category of standardized documents drawn up by administrative institutions of the state. They are different in a broad and narrow sense. Broadly speaking, they embrace both laws governing state administration enacted by institutions of state power, and rules and regulations governing state administration formulated by institutions of state administration. The latter are based on the Constitution and laws within their functions and powers. Narrowly speaking, they are administrative rules and regulations formulated by administrative institutions of the state according to law. Our discussion here involves only administrative rules and regulations, which form an important part of China's legal system.

As soon as they come into force, administrative rules and regulations are binding on both state institutions and citizens. Since they result from institutions legally exercising administrative power on behalf of the state, they are binding on all state institutions. They are rules of conduct to guide state institutions in exercising their functions and powers, and in conducting activities. No administration shall adopt measures violating administrative rules and regulations. After the publication of administrative rules and regulations, citizens affected by them can enjoy certain specified rights and take on corresponding duties. No state organization shall infringe upon such rights. Those citizens who fail to discharge their duties shall be punished accordingly.

According to the Constitution, the State Council has the power to lay down administrative rules and regulations.

THE STATE COUNCIL

An administrative institution of the state is one that applies state power to organize and run administrative affairs of the state. Stipulated by law in terms of its function, power and jurisdiction, the State Council is responsible for organizing and managing national political, economic, cultural and defense affairs, and giving unified guidance to national administration. Local institutions of state administration are directly under the leadership of the State Council. They organize and manage political, economic and cultural affairs as well as routine administrative work in areas under their jurisdiction.

The State Council is also known as the Central People's Government. According to the Organic Law of the State Council, the State Council is composed of the premier, vice-premiers, state councilors, ministers in charge of ministries and commissions, the auditor-general and secretary-general. The premier is responsible for leading the State Council. He is assisted by the vice-premiers and state councilors.

The State Council establishes various ministries, commissions, institutions, and offices directly under it according to the functions of different areas of the political economy. This system is built on the principle of a reasonable division of labor, well-delineated duties, simplified bureaucratic structure and ability to facilitate work. Directly under the guidance of the State Council, each institution is responsible for leadership and management of state administrative affairs within a certain area. These various offices functionally exercise the highest administrative power of the state for the State Council.

As China's state administrative system improve, the functions of the State Council and its institutions of power are also perfected. The State Council's predecessor was the Government Administration Council established in the early years of the People's Republic. At that time, there were thirty ministries, commissions, institutes, administrations and banks. There were also the Political and Law Committee, Finance and Economy Committee, Culture and Education Committee, and People's

Supervisory Committee, which ranked between the Government Administration Council and the ministries. The first three committees gave guidance to the ministries, commissions, institutes, administrations and banks respectively. The People's Supervisory Committee was a special institution that kept an eye on government institutions and functionaries to see if they discharged their duties according to law.

In 1954, the first Constitution of New China was promulgated indicating the further systemization of China's highest source of state administration and its functions. The Constitution reorganized the Government Administration Council — a component part of the Central Government — into the State Council. The NPC and the supreme judicial and procuratorial institutions were now independent of the Central Government. The State Planning Commission and the Ministry of Defense were then placed under the leadership of the State Council. In 1954 the State Council had thirty ministries, five commissions, and political, judicial, cultural, educational, financial and trade offices.

The State Council underwent several adjustments in 1955 and 1956. Some ministries, commissions and offices were added while others were dissolved. By 1982, on the eve of structural reform, it had ninety-eight ministries, commissions, institutes, and offices directly under it, and over forty-nine thousand in personnel. Because it was over-staffed to the extreme, the central authorities decided to reform the government structure.

After the 1982 reform, the State Council cut back the number of ministries, commissions and offices by half, and personnel by one-third. Today, it is made up of forty-five ministries or commissions, and fifteen offices directly under it, such as the State Council Office and the Overseas Chinese Affairs Office.

The premier is responsible for the State Council, which has a number of vice-premiers and state councilors. The premier directs the work of the State Council, calls and conducts the standing committee and plenary meetings of the State Council. The ministers are responsible for the ministries and commissions. Each ministry has one minister and two to four vice-ministers. Each commission has one minister, two to four vice-ministers and five to ten committee members. The minister directs the work of the ministry or commission, convenes and conducts meetings, and signs reports and documents to be submitted to the State Council, as well as orders and instructions to be issued to lower levels. The minister is assisted by the vice-ministers. Each office directly under the State Council is led by two to five persons. These offices are in charge of various types of special businesses. The offices help the premier handle special affairs.

According to Article 89 of the Constitution, the State Council exercises the following functions and powers:

—To adopt administrative measures, enact administrative rules and regulations and issue decisions and orders in accordance with the Constitution and statutes;

—To submit proposals to the NPC or its Standing Committee;

—To lay down the tasks and responsibilities of the ministries and commissions of the State Council, to exercise unified leadership over the work of the ministries and commissions, and to direct all other administrative work of a national character that does not fall within the jurisdiction of the ministries and commissions;

—To exercise unified leadership over the work of local institutions of state administration at different levels throughout the country, and to establish the detailed division of functions and powers between the Central Government and the institutions of state administration of provinces, autonomous regions and municipalities directly under the Central Government;

—To draw up and implement the plan for national economic and social development and the state budget;

—To direct and administer economic affairs and urban and rural development;

—To direct and administer affairs of education, science, culture, public health, physical culture and family planning;

—To direct and administer civil affairs, public security, judicial administration, supervision and other related matters;

—To conduct foreign affairs and conclude treaties and agreements with foreign countries;

—To direct and administer the building of national defense;

—To direct and administer affairs concerning the nationalities, to safeguard the equal rights of minority nationalities and the right to autonomy of the national autonomous regions;

—To protect the legitimate rights and interests of Chinese nationals residing abroad and to protect the lawful rights and interests of returned overseas Chinese and of the family members of Chinese nationals residing abroad;

— To alter or annul inappropriate orders, directives and regulations issued by the ministries or commissions;

—To alter or annul inappropriate decisions and orders issued by local institutions of state administration at different levels;

—To approve the geographic division of provinces, autonomous regions and municipalities directly under the Central Government, and to approve the establishment and geographic division of autonomous prefectures, counties, autonomous counties, and cities;

—To decide on the enforcement of martial law in parts of provinces, autonomous regions and municipalities directly under the Central Government;

—To examine and decide on the size of administrative institutions and, in accordance with the law, to appoint, remove and train administrative officials, appraise their work, and reward or punish them; and

—To exercise such other functions and powers as may be assigned by the NPC or its Standing Committee.

As the highest source of state administration, the State Council enjoys extensive power for administrating the state. One of its vital powers vested by the Constitution and laws is to enact administrative rules and regulations.

INSTITUTIONS TO ENACT
ADMINISTRATIVE RULES AND PROCEDURE

In the course of organizing and directing national administrative work, the State Council enacts administrative rules and regulations according to the Constitution and laws. It also regulates relations between administrative institutions of the state, as well as relations between them and other state institutions, social groups and citizens. This helps it direct effectively and coordinate the work of all ministries. This is an important function of the State Council, and is essential to the state.

During the early years of the People's Republic, the Organic Law of the Central People's Government enacted on the basis of the Common Program of the CPPCC stipulated that to carry out the Common Program, state laws, and administrative policies of the Central Government, the Government Administration Council might issue resolutions and orders and have the right to alter or annul decisions and orders published by ministries, commissions, institutes, administrations, banks or local governments at different levels that contravened state laws or resolutions and orders of the Government Administration Council. Moreover, the Government Administration Council was vested with the power of enacting administrative rules and regulations. To ensure that it could institutionally exercise the power of enacting administrative rules and regulations, the Government Administration Council established a special Law Committee. The Law Committee took on the power of enacting administrative rules and regulations.

Later, the Government Administration Council was reorganized into the State Council. On November 8, 1954, with the approval of the NPC Standing Committee, the State Council instituted a Law Administration on the basis of the former Law Committee. As an office directly under the State Council, the Law Administration was specially responsible for administering the legislative work of the State Council. It sorted out various administrative rules and regulations established by the former Government Administration Council and its subordinate departments, and drafted new administrative rules and regulations according to instructions of the State Council.

In the early period of the Law Administration, it had five groups in charge of drafting, examining, sorting out and compiling rules and regulations for political, judicial, cultural, educational, industrial, labor, financial, commercial, communications, agricultural and foreign affairs. It established a Legal History Research Room and a Translators and Compilers Room to study and gather historical and foreign legislation and administration.

After sorting out administrative rules and regulations, the

Law Administration found that the Government Administration Council had done a great deal of work for administrative legislation. In five years between the founding of the People's Republic and 1954, the Central Government, the Government Administration Council, ministries, commissions and large administrative regions published more than thirty-five hundred administrative rules and regulations, including two hundred and thirty issued by the Government Administration Council.

On the basis of plans for enacting rules and regulations submitted by the ministries to the State Council, the Law Administration worked out an overall plan for examining and drafting administrative rules and regulations. After the Law Administration had evaluated the experience of enacting administrative rules and regulations, the Executive Meeting of the State Council approved the General Organizational Regulations for the Law Administration of the State Council on November 19, 1955. This step confirmed the tasks of the Law Administration. The General Organizational Regulations defined the chief tasks of the Law Administration as follows:

—Examining the drafts of administrative rules and regulations assigned by the State Council;

—Drafting administrative rules and regulations according to the instructions of the State Council;

—Sorting out and compiling administrative rules and regulations promulgated by the State Council; and

—Performing other related legal work assigned by the State Council.

As the administrative rules and regulations drafted by the ministries and commissions involved specialized knowledge of trade and law, the late Premier Zhou Enlai instructed the ministries and commissions to establish their respective legal institutions to help the Law Administration investigate whether the drafted rules and regulations violated state laws and current rules and regulations, and to sort out and compile the related rules and regulations of the respective ministries and commissions.

The State Council attached importance to the Law Administration, which was guaranteed by a system of related institutions. The effective measures for administrative legislation put the miscellaneous and troublesome administrative work of the state on a regular and systematic track. This enhanced the development of political, economic and cultural affairs at that time. It helped the state surmount numerous obstacles in those early days, unravel the terrible state of affairs left by the Kuomintang, and achieve great success in national economic construction.

Since the overthrow of the Lin Biao and Jiang Qing counterrevolutionary cliques, and the Third Plenary Session of the Eleventh CPC Congress, China has strengthened its socialist legal system and brought order out of chaos. The work of enacting administrative rules and regulations has attracted growing attention. On the basis of the former Law Administration, the State Council has enlarged the size of the legal establishment and improved its structure. It has promoted the Law Administration to the General Law Administration with a financial, economic and foreign trade department, an agricultural and forestry department, an industrial and communications department, a supervisory department and a political and judicial department. The five departments are to examine and draft administrative rules and regulations for the respective ministries and commissions. There is also a research room in charge of the study and collecting of materials, and an office to do related daily routine. All this has strengthened administrative legislative work.

As it perfects administrative legislation, China puts the enactment procedure of administrative legislation high on its agenda. For many years administrative legislative work has gradually followed a systematic track, although there is still no specific legislative procedure for enacting administrative rules and regulations. Past practice shows that the procedure for China's administrative legislation can be divided into the following stages:

Drafting administrative rules and regulations Institutions other than state administrative ones may draft administrative rules and regulations for this type of work is not considered legislation. Drafting is also neither fixed nor restricted to particular institutions. Nevertheless, the draft must be recognized by the related legislative institution before it can come into force. Generally speaking, China's administrative rules and regulations are drafted by related specialized ministries and commissions, and submitted to the Law Administration of the State Council for examination.

Examining administrative rules and regulations At this crucial stage of administrative legislation, the Law Administration is authorized by the State Council to examine the drafts of administrative rules and regulations submitted by ministries and commissions. Only those rules and regulations confirming to the stipulations of law can be established. Administrative rules and regulations in China must meet the following requirements;

—The institution enacting administrative rules and regulations must have corresponding legislative power;

— The administrative rules and regulations enacted shall not overstep the functions and power of that institution;

—The substance of the administrative rules and regulations shall not contravene the Constitution, laws and relevant administrative rules and regulations; and

— The enactment of administrative rules and regulations must be a formal legal act. It must be completed in written form, signed by the leader of the institution and dated. Important administrative rules and regulations should be passed by the Executive Meeting of the State Council.

Publishing administrative rules and regulations Adopted administrative rules and regulations shall be officially published in the name of the State Council. In special circumstances, they could be officially published in the name of ministries and commissions according to decisions made by the Law Administration or the Executive Meeting of the State Council. Only after they have been officially published can administrative rules and regulations become legally effective.

Altering, withdrawing, or annulling administrative rules and regulations If any administrative rules and regulations turn out to be against the law or inappropriate after publication, the State Council could take administrative measures to alter or withdraw them. Withdrawn rules and regulations are considered legally void, *nunc pro tunc*. In special cases, they could lose legal validity from the date of withdrawal.

If circumstances have changed, the State Council can annul

administrative rules and regulations that have been published. It annuls them in either of the following two ways: **A.** Direct annulment, i.e., the State Council annuls them by issuing administrative rules and regulations stipulated in explicit terms; **B.** Indirect annulment, i.e., later laws and administrative rules and regulations override the former rules and regulations according to the principle of new rules repealing old ones.

Compiling and sorting out administrative rules and regulations To ensure that the adopted administrative rules and regulations are carried out well and that administrative legislation is gradually systematized and rationalized on the basis of experience, the Law Administration must regularly compile and sort out administrative rules and regulations, a task it has fulfilled with considerable success. It has already completed the compilation of administrative rules and regulations adopted since the founding of the People's Republic. This gives great impetus to China's administrative and legislative work.

SUBSTANCE AND SCOPE OF ADMINISTRATIVE RULES AND REGULATIONS ENACTED BY THE STATE COUNCIL

The purpose of enacting administrative rules and regulations is to eradicate all maladies resulting from chaotic management, such as an overstaffed structure, lack of definition of duties and power, improper reward and punishment, procrastination, and inefficiency. In its report to the Third Session of the Fifth NPC, the State Council stated that it would organize special personnel to enact a system of administrative rules and regulations. These would define the functions and powers of each ministry and department, the principle of exercising functions and powers, and methods of handling special questions. Such administrative rules and regulations would help reduce the huge amount of reports, and authorize the ministries and commissions to solve numerous problems independently, according to their specified functions and principles.

Without a stable system of administrative rules and regulations as a legal basis, the ministries, commissions and localities would write reports for instructions whenever a problem crops up, leading to the circulation of inordinately large numbers of official documents. Work efficiency would be at stake and the growth of bureaucracy encouraged. Hence, the purpose of strengthening administrative legislation is to raise the administrative level of the state as a whole.

Large-scale administration suggests that China's highest institution of state administration should enact an enormous number of rules and regulations. Nevertheless, its purpose is to raise the administrative efficiency of the whole state. Hence, there is a need for definition in substance and scope to the rules and regulations. The administrative rules and regulations enacted by the State Council since the founding of the People's Republic can be broken down into the following five major categories:

Those stipulating work systems for the personnel of state organizations, and building up a strong contingent of administrative cadres The state personnel are concrete executors of state policies and laws. Personnel administration is a duty of the administrative institutions and a prerequisite to accomplishing the tasks and functions of state administration. Without a strict and practical cadre system, it is hard to carry out the policies and laws of the state. Therefore, using administrative rules and regulations to legalize the system of cadre assessment, promotion, reward, punishment, recall and retirement is a basic guarantee for bringing the personnel's initiative into play, for employing talented persons reasonably, and for raising work efficiency.

Those defining the rights and duties of state institutions in administrative activities and their relationship with other state organizations, social groups, businesses, institutions and citizens The administrative affairs of the state are multifarious and disorderly. They involve politics, economy, national defense, communications, public security, civil affairs, the press, physical culture, health, science, education and family planning. Apart from those governed by civil law, economic law and labor law, most of the other affairs come within the scope of administrative rules and regulations. For example, the enacted Urban Communications Rules, Census Registration Regulations and Industrial and Commercial Enterprises Registration and Control Regulations, etc., specify the rights and duties of the related departments in their administrative activities and in their relations with other state organizations, social groups and citizens. This would help the departments and organizations coordinate with each other, each doing its duty and all forming an organic system of administration. This clarifies and specifies the extensive legal relationships between the administrative organizations and other state organizations, social groups, businesses, institutions and citizens. How should each administrative department conduct its work? What rights and duties do the related departments and persons have? All these questions are answered in the administrative rules and regulations. China's administrative rules and regulations are relatively perfect in this respect. As they are characterized by specialization, they are usually drafted by the respective departments in charge, and submitted to the State Council for examination and approval. In examining such administrative rules and regulations, the State Council pays attention to the coordination and balance between the departments.

Those defining the organizational structure and limits of power of departments of the People's Government and self-management mass organizations at the grassroots The State Council has enacted a large number of such administrative rules and regulations which have brought excellent results in practice. For example, the City Residents' Committee Organic Rules stipulate that the committee should be established according to the circumstances of civilian residence and districts controlled by the police. The chief task of the committee is to lead the masses in public security work, in mediating disputes between residents, and in promoting public welfare. The Organic Rules for the Office of the Neighborhood Committee stipulate that the office is an agency of an urban district or a city without districts. Each office has a director and a number of staff members according to the size of the district or city and the amount of work. When necessary, it can have a deputy director. The office administers affairs assigned by the people's committee of the city or urban district.

The Provincial Organic Regulations for the Public Security Committee specify that the committee is composed of three to ten persons including one director and one or two deputy directors. Its duty is to arrest active criminals and those wanted by the law and send them to the public security offices without the right to interrogate, detain, or punish them. For inactive criminals, it has the right to make investigations, keep them under surveillance, and report them to the public security offices. It has no right to arrest, detain, search, and otherwise punish them. It has the right to urge the masses to maintain public order, to oversee criminals doing penal work and report their conduct to the public security offices. But it has no right to detain, punish or expel the criminals under surveillance. In case of a criminal incident, the committee should help the police maintain order and secure the crime scene for inspection by the police.

The Provisional General Organic Rules for the People's Mediation Committees stipulate that the committee is composed of three to eleven persons. The committee mediates settlements of general civil disputes and light criminal cases.

There are other administrative rules and regulations such as the Working Regulations for the State Planning Commission, Working Regulations for the Planning Commissions of People's Committee at Local Levels, General Organic Regulations for the Labor Ministry, General Organic Regulations for the Expert Administration of the State Council, and General Organic Regulations for the Law Administration of the State Council.

These administrative rules and regulations enacted since the founding of the People's Republic specify the organization, functions, powers, working procedures, size of staff and methods of administration for departments of the central and local governments. They clarify the duties and limits of power of different departments and give a great impetus to the work of government institutions at all levels. As time passes and government institutions reform, however, some of these administrative rules and regulations no longer meet present needs. For instance, some departments still have no organic rules to base their work on. They argue back and forth, and create a serious situation. To solve these problems, the State Council is studying how to enact new rules and regulations, and how to amend and perfect current ones.

Enacting various economic management rules and regulations
Rules and regulations for economic management are important

tools of a socialist state for directing and managing economy. The State Council has promulgated large numbers of rules and regulations for economic management, eliminating the practice of managing economy by purely administrative means. This has played a tremendous part in improving economic relations between state organizations, businesses, institutions, industries run by rural townships and towns, and citizens. These rules and regulations account for the greatest number of China's administrative rules and regulations. By means of the rules and regulations for economic management, the state exercises the function of organizing and managing the national economy.

To meet the need of economic reforms and opening to the outside world, China has made rapid progress in economic legislation over the past few years. Between 1979 and 1985, the State Council approved and promulgated more than 350 economic management rules and regulations including the Provisional Regulations for Encouraging Economic Associations, Provisional Regulations for Initiating and Protecting Socialist Competition, Foreign Exchange Control Regulations, Stipulations About Certain Problems for Developing Commune and Brigade Businesses (tentative draft), and Tentative Regulations for Capital Construction Loans.

To ensure success in economic legislation, the State Council established the Economic Rules and Regulations Research Center in 1981 to study the legislative work of enacting economic rules and regulations. The center also instructs, organizes and coordinates the ministries and commissions in enacting and amending economic rules and regulations, and develops a unified plan to accomplish these ends. Many departments of the State Council have also established special agencies in charge of such work. For example, the State Planning Commission has instituted a rules and regulations office, the State Economic Commission a rules and regulations bureau, the Ministry of Finance a law department, and the Ministry of Foreign Economic Relations and Trade a rules and regulations department.

Enacting administrative rules and regulations for the military Military administration is an essential part of the administration of the state. Military administrative rules and regulations are one of the legal means by which the state administers

65

the establishment of the armed forces and its needs in terms of equipment, education, training, and scientific research. The organizational system of China's armed forces is divided into military and administrative parts. The Central Military Commission leads all armed forces in China. It has the power to command and deploy the entire armed forces. The State Council leads and administers national defense building. Military administrative rules and regulations promulgated by the State Council generally refer to plans for enhancing national defense and to corresponding administrative work.

According to the Organic Law of the State Council, the ministries and commissions should report their general and specific policies, plans and essential administrative measures they intend to adopt, to the State Council for instruction. It is up to the State Council to make decisions. According to the decisions of the State Council, the ministries and commissions can, within their respective functions and powers, issue orders, instructions and rules. Once discussed and adopted by the Executive Meeting of the State Council or a plenary meeting, these orders, instructions and rules become administrative rules and regulations enacted by the State Council.

CHAPTER 5

Local Institutions of State Power and Administrative Rules and Regulations

The people's congresses of provinces, autonomous regions, municipalities directly under the Central Government, and their standing committees are China's local institutions of state power. According to stipulations of the Constitution, they have the power to enact and promulgate local rules and regulations to suit specific local circumstances while meeting practical needs on condition that these rules and regulations do not violate the Constitution, and laws and administrative rules and regulations. Local rules and regulations, including autonomous ones, are inseparable component parts of China's unified legal system.

The Constitution or the National People's Congress vests the local people's congresses and their standing committees with the power to enact local rules and regulations. This plays a vital part in strengthening local legal system, in improving China's legal system as a whole, and is suiting the special circumstances of a vast country with abundant resources, but with different levels of development in the social, political and economic arenas in various localities.

LOCAL PEOPLE'S CONGRESSES

China applies a four-level system of institutions of state power. The NPC is at the top, the highest source of state power. At the second level are people's congresses of provinces, autonomous regions, and municipalities directly under the Central Government as local institutions of state power at the provincial level. At the third and county level are the people's congresses of autonomous prefectures, counties, autonomous counties, cities and urban districts. At the lowest and township level are the people's congresses of townships, national townships and towns.

Before 1979, only the local people's congresses exercised local state power on behalf of the Chinese people. Therewere no standing committees of the local people's congresses. Their functions and powers were executed by the respective people's governments. As the democracy and legal system of the state developed and the system of state political power improved, the local people's congresses acquired a more and more important position in the system of state power. The political line, general and specific policies, and the Constitution and laws of the Central Government must be carried out by the people's congresses at all levels to ensure their nationwide implementation. But the people's congress meets only once a year. Consequently, it was inadequate to depend on the people's congress alone to ensure the enforcement of the Constitution and laws, and to discuss and decide on major issues in the concerned administrative areas. Besides, there was a great deal of routine work for the local institution of state power. All this called for the establishment of a special permanent body to carry on part of the duties of the people's congress when it was not in session. This would eradicate the maladies caused by the local people's government's assuming the functions and powers of the people's congress.

The combination of an institution of power with an administrative institution, however, was thought to be disadvantageous both to the work of the administrative institution and to the supervision exercised by the institution of power over the administrative institution. Therefore, the Fifth NPC amended the organic laws of local people's congresses and local people's governments in 1979, and ruled that people's congresses at and above the county level should establish standing committees. The people's congress standing committees were to organize people's deputies to carry on regular activities. This ensured the continual work of the local institutions of state power at all levels and strengthened the local political power of the state. As the

68

system of people's congresses has developed, the establishment of people's congress standing committees in townships and towns has now been put on the agenda and consideration is pending.

According to present Chinese laws, the local people's congress standing committee at the county level or above is a permanent body of the people's congress at the same level. It is responsible to and reports its work to the people's congress.

The people's congress standing committee at the county level or above is composed of a chairman, some vice-chairmen and a number of members elected from the people's deputies by the people's congress at the same level. No one on the standing committee shall hold post in any of the administrative, judicial or procuratorial institutions of the state. Anyone who holds such a post must submit one's resignation to the standing committee.

The local people's congresses at all levels and their standing committees enjoy extensive power including the following:

Decision-making power   They have the right to discuss and decide on major political, economic, cultural, educational, public health, civil and nationality affairs of their respective administrative areas, as well as to examine and approve local plans, budgets, and final accounts for the national economy.

Power of supervision   They are vested with the power of legal supervision and work supervision. They have the right to ensure the observance and enforcement of the state Constitution, laws, decrees and policies as well as the resolutions of people's congresses at higher levels, and to ensure the implementation of state economic plans and budgets. They have the right to amend or annul inappropriate decisions and orders of the people's governments at the same levels and to listen to and examine the working reports of the people's courts and the people's procuratorates at the same levels.

Power of personnel appointment and removal   They elect or decide on the choice of leaders of the people's governments, people's courts and people's procuratorates at the same levels according to the procedure of law.

Apart from enjoying the above-mentioned powers, the people's congresses and their standing committees at the provincial level, people's congress standing committees of cities that are seats of provincial or autonomous regional people's governments and of major cities approved by the State Council, as well as people's congresses of autonomous regions, autonomous counties and autonomous prefectures, enjoy corresponding legislative power or the power of enacting administrative rules and regulations. Comprising the entire content of China's local legal system, they are an essential component part of the national unified legal system.

LEGISLATIVE POWER OF LOCAL PEOPLE'S CONGRESSES AND THEIR STANDING COMMITTEES

Among the local people's congresses and their standing committees, the power of enacting administrative rules and regulations is vested in only the people's congresses and their standing committees at the provincial level, the city level if the cities are seats of provincial or autonomous regional people's governments, and of major cities approved by the State Council. Power is also vested in people's congresses of autonomous prefectures and autonomous counties. No other institution shall have the power to enact local and autonomous rules and regulations.

According to the stipulations of the present Chinese laws, the people's congresses of provinces, autonomous regions and municipalities directly under the Central Government can enact and promulgate local rules and regulations to meet the specific circumstances and practical needs of their respective administrative areas. They report to the NPC Standing Committee and the State Council and these rules and regulations cannot contravene the state Constitution, laws, policies and decrees. When the people's congresses are not in session, their standing committees can act likewise.

The people's congress standing committees of major cities approved by the State Council and of cities that are seats of provincial or autonomous regional people's governments can draft local rules and regulations to meet urban needs, submit them to the provincial or autonomous regional people's congresses for examination and enactment, and report them to the NPC Standing Committee and the State Council. Practice has shown that the power of drafting rules and regulations would easily bring discord in the procedure of examination and approval.

At present, the Commission of Legislative Affairs of the NPC Standing Committee is studying how to make specific amendments to the organic laws of local people's congresses and local people's governments. It plans to vest the power of enacting local rules and regulations in cities that are seats of provincial or autonomous regional people's governments, as well as in major cities approved by the State Council. The reason is that these cities are political, economic and cultural centers of their areas, and their rate of development far exceeds that of the surrounding rural country. Therefore, to implement state laws, policies, and administrative rules and regulations, these cities must be able to enact, with authority, rules and regulations concerning the vital and urgent problems in society and in their economy. These problems may crop up in municipal administration, environmental protection, communications and transportation, and economic circulation. The vesting of such power will step up the development of the cities, and help them generate political, economic and cultural growth in surrounding areas.

The people's congresses of national autonomous regions have the right to enact autonomous regulations and separate regulations in the light of local political, economic and cultural characteristics. Such regulations shall be reported to the NPC Standing Committee for approval before coming into force. Autonomous regulations and separate regulations formulated by autonomous prefectures or autonomous counties shall be reported to the people's congress standing committee of the respective province or autonomous region for approval before coming into force, and to the NPC Standing Committee for the record.

The legislative power of the people's congresses and their standing committees of provinces, autonomous regions or municipalities directly under the Central Government, of cities that are seats of provincial or autonomous regional people's governments, of major cities approved by the State Council, or of national autonomous prefectures and counties, is all characterized by a local and supplementary nature. This legislative power focuses on problems that require legislation for their resolution in the specific administrative area, and where there are no fixed state rules and regulations to refer to as guidelines. According to the stipulations of Chinese laws and legislative practice over the past few years, the legislative power of the people's congresses and their standing committees at the provincial level is demonstrated in the following four aspects:

Detailed regulations for law enforcement To ensure the enforcement of the Constitution and laws, the provincial people's congresses and their standing committees lay down detailed regulations and measures according to state laws in the light of the actual circumstances of their respective administrative areas. For instance, according to the stipulations of the Election Law and the Criminal Procedure Law of the People's Republic of China, the provincial people's congresses or their standing committees have established detailed regulations for the Election Law, and measures for enforcing the Criminal Procedure Law, etc. Such local rules and regulations must embody the following features:

They must be based on the stipulations of state laws without any changes or adaptations; and

They must ensure the enforcement of laws.

Autonomous power of enacting rules and regulations The people's congresses of national autonomous regions have the power to enact and promulgate autonomous regulations and separate regulations in the light of the political, economic and cultural characteristics of the local nationality. China has more than fifty national minorities. The legislation of national autonomous regions is an essential part of local rules and regulations. Such local rules and regulations primarily involve the following three aspects:

National autonomous regulations They are rules and regulations administering national affairs, integrating the power vested by the Constitution and laws with the characteristics of the local nationalities. They cover many aspects focusing on the autonomy of minority nationalities.

Separate regulations They are enacted by the institutions of power in national autonomous regions to solve particular

72

problems and to protect the special interests of the local nationalities.

Flexible measures and supplementary regulations   They are adopted to carry out state laws in the light of local circumstances. Although autonomous legislative power has a greater right to make decisions and can make certain adaptations of the state laws, the adaptations must be aimed at ensuring the enforcement of laws and must conform to the basic principles of state laws.

Local power of enacting rules and regulations   This is the power to enact local rules and regulations suited to the local political, economic, cultural and public affairs concerning the vital interests of the people. This is also a power vested by the NPC and its Standing Committee to enact regulations for special economic zones. Local rules and regulations are decisions and regulations made by the institutions of power of provinces, autonomous regions and municipalities directly under the Central Government in the light of local circumstances and local characteristics. Often, the issues involved are inconspicuous from a national point of view. Lacking unified state laws for reference, urgent enactment of regulations by local authorities are both necessary and proper.

Vesting the power of enacting rules and regulations   The NPC and its Standing Committee vest the provincial people's congresses and their standing committees with the power of enacting separate economic rules and regulations for the special economic zones they control. The special economic zones signify a new type of economic administration that has appeared in the course of China's economic reforms. The system of special economic zones embodies open economic policies in a number of coastal areas. Those policies involve special taxes, loans, greater imports and exports where they will help enhance economic development. The Fifth NPC Standing Committee has done much to make construction in special economic zones a success and to help economic management meet its needs there. It has vested the people's congresses of Guangdong and Fujian provinces and their standing committees with the power of enacting various economic rules and regulations for their special economic zones. These measures are in accordance with the principles of related

73

state laws, decrees and policies in the light of specific circumstances and actual needs of the zones. The provincial people's congresses and their standing committees shall report the separate rules and regulations they enact to the NPC Standing Committee and the State Council.

As a result, the Fifth People's Congress Standing Committee of Guangdong Province in 1981 adopted the Interim Provisions of the Shenzhen Special Economic Zone for Land Management, Interim Provisions for Labor and Wage Management in Enterprises in the Special Economic Zones in Guangdong Province, Interim Provisions for the Registration and Administration of Enterprises in the Special Economic Zones in Guangdong Province, and Interim Provisions of Special Economic Zones for the Control of Personnel Entering or Leaving China. Similarly, the Fifth People's Congress of Fujian Province adopted the Regulations for the Xiamen Special Economic Zone in Fujian Province, Regulations for Labor Control of the Xiamen Special Economic Zone in Fujian Province, Regulations Governing the Use of Land by Overseas Businessmen in the Xiamen Special Economic Zone in Fujian Province, and Regulations for Registering Enterprises in the Xiamen Special Economic Zone in Fujian Province.

These local rules and regulations of special economic zones are legal standards governing the rights and duties of both foreign and Chinese investors in their economic cooperation or technological and trade exchanges. They are legal guarantee for cooperation in China's special economic zones.

In short, all types of local rules and regulations enacted by the people's congresses and their standing committees of provinces, autonomous regions, municipalities directly under the Central Government, cities that are seats of provincial or autonomous regional people's governments, major cities approved by the State Council and national autonomous areas have the following characteristics:

—All are products of integrating the basic principles of the Constitution and laws with the specific circumstances of the respective administrative areas.

—All must be enacted within the limits of legal power and shall be effective in the respective administrative areas.

74

—And all shall be reported to the NPC Standing Committee.

These characteristics embody China's unified legislative system with two orders and three divisions.

PRINCIPLES AND PROCEDURE FOR ENACTING LOCAL RULES AND REGULATIONS

The law vests local institutions of state power with the right to enact local rules and regulations. This helps bring the initiative of local institutions of state power into full play, so that they can play a dynamic role in administering state affairs and ensuring the practical enforcement of the state Constitution and laws. Nevertheless, to uphold the unity of the state legal system and the seriousness of state laws, the local institutions of state power, in enacting rules and regulations, must follow certain principles and procedures, and accept direct supervision by superior institutions of state power.

—In enacting all kinds of local rules and regulations, the local institutions of state power must adhere to the state Constitution and laws. They shall enact them on the basis of the guiding principle of the Constitution and laws, and not violate it. Even the language of the local rules and regulations shall be modeled after the standardized language of the Constitution and laws. No violation of the relevant stipulations of the Constitution and laws shall be allowed.

In the past few years, the local institutions of state power have been able to adhere to the stipulations of the Constitution and laws in handling related matters. For example, when the Beijing Municipal People's Congress Standing Committee was drafting the Provisional Organic Regulations for Villagers' Committees in Beijing Municipality, many cadres on the standing committees of county people's congresses and of township governments strongly demanded that the regulations specify the right of the township government to lead the villagers' committee. Some even demanded that the villagers' committee be defined as grassroots political power in China's rural country, equivalent to the village government in the times of the

Anti-Japanese War. Nevertheless, the Constitution says the villagers' committee is only a mass self-management organization, not an agency of the township people's government. The relationship between the township people's government and the villagers' committee is one of instruction, not leadership. The Beijing Municipal People's Congress adhered to the stipulations of the Constitution and wrote that "Villagers' committee carries out work under the instruction of the people's government of township, national township or town."

When the Beijing Municipal People's Congress Standing Committee drafted the Resolution for Protecting the Legitimate Rights and Interests of Women and Children, many suggested that a third person intervening in the affairs of a married couple and splitting up the family should be punished as an adulterer. The Beijing Municipal People's Congress Standing Committee, however, held that no local rules and regulations can override the state's unified Criminal Law and define new crimes. This avoided discord or contradiction between state laws and local rules and regulations and upheld the unity, solemnity and authority of state laws.

—In enacting local rules and regulations, local institutions of state power must proceed from the actual circumstances of the locality and take local characteristics into account. Local rules and regulations are characterized by their local nature. They are aimed at resolving vital problems in related administrative areas. Therefore, in enacting local rules and regulations, the local institution of state power must conduct investigations and studies, and seek truth from facts to embody local characteristics.

In such a vast country as China, political, economic and cultural developments are not always equal. In drafting and examining local rules and regulations, one must know the exact state of local political, economic and cultural developments, and existing problems. One must take a scientific approach and correctly distinguish between advanced areas, general areas and backward areas, between town and country. One must have a clear-cut idea of local structural reforms and strategy for economic development, and ascertain the special contradictions within the locality. One must base one's work on the actual local situation. Local institutions of state power should enact rules and regulations only when special circumstances make it necessary and no related state law exists to provide guidance or enforcement of state law would present a great difficulty to the locality. For example, the People's Congress Standing Committee of Hunan Province has laid down the Protective Measures for the Safety of Mines in Hunan Province because there was no such state law and the question of the safety of provincial mines was becoming serious.

Apart from adhering to the above-mentioned principle, the local institutions of state power must follow strict legislative procedure. Unlike legislation enacted by the NPC and its Standing Committee, local legislation must be carefully restricted by procedure to ensure the unity and solemnity of state legislation as a whole. In addition to state laws stipulating procedure for local legislation, such as the Organic Law for Localities, many provinces and municipalities have formulated special rules for adopting procedures in enacting local rules and regulations.

Legislative procedure not only must include the process of proposal, examination, adopting and publication, but must also be reported to the NPC Standing Committee and the State Council. The NPC and its Standing Committee have the right to legal supervision according to the procedure of supervision, and to annul local rules, regulations, or resolutions that contravene the state Constitution, laws and administrative rules and regulations. The local institutions of state power should accept the guidance and supervision of the NPC and its Standing Committee in enacting local rules and regulations to ensure the harmonious development of state legislation as a whole.

CHAPTER 6

Judicial System and Its Institutions

Since the founding of the People's Republic, the development of China's judicial system has been consistent only in its fluctuations. The judicial system and its institutions, however, did develop rapidly following the conclusion of the "cultural revolution," and, in particular, after the Third Plenary Session of the Eleventh CPC Congress in 1978.

China has, over the past few years, promulgated and amended a number of laws and decrees including the Criminal Procedure Law, the Civil Procedure Law, the Organic Law of the People's Courts and the Organic Law of the People's Procuratorates, and provisional regulations concerning lawyers and public notaries. In March 1978, the Fifth NPC decided to re—establish procuratorates in China. In September 1979, the Fifth NPC Standing Committee decided at its Eleventh Session to establish the Ministry of Justice so as to institutionalize the administration of justice. The State Council issued a circular in the same year demanding that administrative institutions of justice be established at different levels in all parts of the country with the institutionalization of assistants of justice at the district and township levels.

In June 1983, the Sixth NPC decided at its First Session to set up the Ministry of State Security to take over the investigation of certain kinds of cases from the Ministry of Public Security. In April of the same year, the State Council decided to place the work of reform through labor, a task of the Ministry of Public Security, under the control of the Ministry of Justice. In November 1984, the Sixth NPC Standing Committee adopted at its Eighth Session the Decision on Establishment of Maritime Courts at Port Cities, thus further strengthening the country's judicial system and judicial institutions.

In short, China's judicial system and judicial institutions have been steadily improved over the past few years, along with the gradual strengthening of the country's socialist legal system which is based on the Constitution, the fundamental law of the country. So as the socialist commodity economy grows and socialist democracy improves, China's judicial system, which has unique Chinese characteristics, will also be strengthened.

CHARACTERISTICS

China's judicial system is different both in theory and practice from that of the Western liberal nations. While the latter exists within the context of the separation of powers, China's has a unitary people's congress system. Nevertheless, in China, as in the West, the judiciary is an important part of the state government.

The people's congress system in China is the foundation on which state organization is built. It is, however, different from the parliamentary system in that the people's congress system merges legislative with executive power. State power is unitary instead of plural, while there is a division of labor and responsibilities for sectors of government under the unified guidance of state power, i.e., the people's congress. The NPC is China's highest instrumentality of state power, while all others such as the State Council (the executive), the People's Court (the judiciary) and the Procuratorate are created and supervised by, and held accountable to it. The same is true in the relationship at different levels between the local people's congress and the local judiciary.

China's judiciary is composed of the people's courts, people's procuratorates, public security, state security, and administrative institutions of justice. People's courts are state institutions of adjudication and independently exercise the power of adjudication. People's procuratorates are state institutions for supervising implementation of laws and decrees. They exercise independently procuratorial power and are responsible for approving arrests, instituting prosecutions, and supervising the activities of judicial institutions. Public security branches are extensions of state security offices and are responsible for maintaining social and public order and state security, and for conducting investigations, arrests and preliminary hearings in criminal cases. The administrative institutions of justice are functional departments under the people's governments at different levels. They supervise the administration of justice including that of prisons and reform through labor. Leaders of public security, state security, and administrative offices of justice are appointed by standing committees of the people's congresses at different levels upon nomination of related people's governments. In judicial work, public security, procuratorates and administrative offices of justice operate according to their division of labor, coordinate and curb each other so as to ensure correct and effective implementation of state laws and decrees.

In short, the characteristics of China's judicial system can be summarized as follows:

Uniformity China's judicial system upholds the principle of uniformity, i.e., application of unified judicial powers, laws and decrees, and unified judicial system. China's judicial powers encompass the power of adjudication, procuratorial power, the power of investigation and administrative power of justice. In the light of the state Constitution and other laws, these powers are exercised respectively by the courts, procuratorates, public security institutions (including institutions of state security) and administrative institutions of justice under the unified leadership of institutions of state power, i.e., people's congresses at different levels. No other organizations or individuals are entitled to use these powers. A unified legal system is in place throughout the country. Courts and procuratorates are directly responsible and report to such state institutions of power as people's congresses at their corresponding level. Organizationally, public security, state security, and administrative institutions of justice are under various governments.

Independence China's judicial institutions exercise their powers independently according to law. But this independence is different from the "judicial independence" of the Western liberal democracies. The judicial institutions in China function under the unified leadership of state institutions of power. Therefore, judicial independence exists only in regard to other institutions of state power.

For instance, courts exercising judicial authority and procuratorates exercising procuratorial power are organizationally independent from administrative departments. Judicial and procuratorial personnel are elected, appointed, or dismissed by state institutions of power at the corresponding level, so they do not enjoy life tenure. The investigators and administrative personnel of justice are appointed or dismissed by administrative institutions. All personnel in the judiciary and procuratorate enjoy the same treatment in welfare and retirement benefits same as other governmental personnel.

Crime prevention first in judicial work To maintain social order and reduce criminality, China's judiciary carries out the principle of prevention first. Proceeding from China's social and economic conditions, a whole range of successful measures have been developed which have reduced criminal cases and are referred to as "comprehensive treatment of social and public order." By "comprehensive treatment," we mean to mobilize all citizens in an effort to eliminate the root causes of the crime and eliminate the social and economic causes within the environment which creates it. The specific measures are:

Mobilizing the mass organizations of workers, youths and women, as well as schools, cultural and publicity institutions These sectors will disseminate general knowledge of the law among the people in cooperation with the judicial institutions, educate the people in communist ethics, foster socialist legality and good social conduct, and thus promote socialist civilization. These are fundamental to reducing and preventing crime.

Establishing and improving the responsibility system for maintaining social and public order All schools, government departments, factories, enterprises and other institutions have introduced a public security responsibility system. This system links closely the workers' maintenance of discipline, and social and public order, with successful on the job performance. This has enabled everyone to show concern for the security work of his or her work unit, creating conditions for reducing the crime rate.

Strengthening legal work at grassroots levels Neighborhood committees and villagers' committees in urban and rural areas are self-governing organizations of the people. Under these organizations there are public security committees and people's mediation committees. All the committee members are elected by the people. They make regular efforts to educate the people in socialist ethics and heighten their consciousness of laws, mediate conflicts, and handle minor criminal offenses.

Disseminating general knowledge of the law among the people so as to enhance legal awareness Government employees especially should be educated so that they can generally handle matters according to the law. This is an important measure for improving general social conduct and reducing criminal offenses.

Providing legal convenience for litigants Aimed at fostering closer ties with the people, this important principle serves the people's interest in many ways. Establishment of the people's courts and the holding of open circuit level trials encourage citizens of that circuit to participate in, and learn from, the operation of the judicial process. Encouraging the use of mediation as an alternative to resolving civil disputes and minor criminal offenses prior to the initiation of formal court proceedings, saves the state and the litigants from the economic cost and burden of time-consuming litigation. Mediation, through the practice of consultation of both parties, allows for resolution of disputes in a fair and lawful manner.

In criminal cases, the cost of litigation has been reduced or eliminated. China does not charge a fee for criminal cases. If the court appoints an attorney to represent the defendant, it will cover the expense. In general, the court does not charge any fees for civil cases with a few exceptions. However, if the civil litigants cannot afford to pay the fees, they can be waived. This procedure guarantees the people's right to litigation. Concurrently, procedure and regulations are simple and easy to understand, making it possible for citizens to exercise their right to litigation.

82

RELATIONSHIPS AMONG
CHINA'S JUDICIAL INSTITUTIONS

According to the Constitution and other relevant laws, people's courts, people's procuratorates and public and state security institutions shall have a division of labor with separate responsibilities. They coordinate and curb each other while conducting criminal proceedings. This process is designed to guarantee effective enforcement of the law.

China's courts, procuratorates, public and state security institutions share the common task of protecting the people. They suppress enemies of the state, punish criminals, safeguard the drive for socialist modernization, and consolidate the people's democratic dictatorship. These are the fundamental goals of China's legal system. China's Constitution and the Criminal Procedure Law also define the scope of the legal system with a specific division of labor. Common tasks and different responsibilities reflect the relationship of mutual cooperation and restriction between the judicial organizations, representing the "three links" of a chain and "three work processes" of an indispensable mechanism. In criminal proceedings, the three stages of investigation, prosecution and adjudication are similar to the three work processes. If public and state security organizations, procuratorates, and courts interact through checks and balances, they will handle criminal cases efficiently, lawfully, expeditiously, and according to humane requirements. Should there be anything wrong with any of the three processes, the entire handling of the case would be adversely affected, damaging the interests of the state and the people. Therefore, the relationship between China's judicial organizations in the division of labor, mutual coordination and restriction is extremely important. It is also a salient feature of China's judicial system.

Division of labor The public and state security organizations, procuratorates, and courts shall perform their functions as prescribed by law and carry out their activities strictly according to their division of labor. In the light of the Constitution and other laws, the people's court is a state judicial institution exercising judicial power on behalf of the state. According to the law, the people's courts shall conduct adjudication independently and are subject only to the law. Only the people's courts are empowered to hold public hearings for both civil and criminal cases. The first paragraph in Article 13 of the Criminal Procedure Law says, "Minor criminal cases that may be handled only upon complaint, and others that do not require the conducting of an investigation, are to be accepted directly by the people's courts, and mediation may be carried out." This means that the people's courts may deal directly with the following two categories of criminal cases:

— Cases that may be handled only upon complaint, including slandering or defaming another person as prescribed in Article 145 of the Criminal Law, and using violence to interfere with the freedom of marriage of others as designated in Article 179 of the same law.

—Minor cases that do not require an investigation, such as committing bigamy as provided for in Article 180 of the Criminal Law, disrupting the marriage of a member of the armed forces on active duty as designated in Article 181, committing the crime of desertion mentioned in Article 183, and committing the crime of disrupting the performance of public service.

The people's procuratorates are state institutions for supervising the enforcement of the laws and exercising their procuratorial power independently. According to the Criminal Procedure Law, the procuratorates are mainly responsible for approving arrest, conducting procuratorial work (including investigation) and initiating public prosecution. The second paragraph of Article 13 of the Criminal Procedure Law stipulates that "Cases involving corruption, violation of the rights of citizens, dereliction of duty, and other cases that the people's procuratorates consider necessary to accept directly are to be filed and investigated by the people's procuratorates, which are to decide whether or not to initiate a public prosecution."

The first three categories of crimes listed above are crimes committed by state personnel who abuse their powers or take advantage of their office. As for other criminal cases that the people's procuratorates consider necessary to accept, no specific provisions have been made. It is necessary for the procuratorates to decide themselves.

The public security institutions are empowered by the state to be responsible for maintaining social order and state security. They are a component of state administration. In the light of the law, public security institutions are primarily responsible for investigating, detaining, conducting preparatory examinations, and effecting arrests in criminal proceedings.

The third paragraph of Article 13 of the Criminal Procedure Law provides that "The investigations of cases other than those provided in the first and second paragraphs are all to be conducted by public security institutions." This means all criminal cases other than those directly accepted by the people's courts, and those investigated by the people's procuratorates, are to be filed and investigated by the people's security institutions. The First Session of the Sixth NPC decided in September 1983 to create an institution of state security to take over the espionage cases from public security. As state security possesses characteristics of its public security counterparts, state security may also exercise powers as stipulated in the state Constitution and other laws. These are powers to conduct investigate, detain, prepare examinations and effect arrests in criminal proceedings.

In handling criminal cases, China's judicial system must have a division of labor with separate responsibilities. Public and state security organizations, procuratorates and courts should cooperate so as to make an accurate and timely assessment of the crimes, and to ensure correct and effective implementation of the law.

Mutual coordination This means that the public and state security organizations, procuratorates and courts should, on the basis of their division of labor, cooperate with and support each other in order to complete their common tasks of preventing crime and administering justice.

Their mutual coordination is demonstrated in the following ways:

—When a public or state security office deems it necessary to make an arrest, it submits a proposal to the people's procuratorate for approval of the arrest. After the people's procuratorate conducts a review of the case, it makes a decision either to approve or disapprove the arrest, or to carry out its own investigation.

—An arrest shall be carried out by a public or state security office.

—In an investigation by a public or state security office, an opinion recommending prosecution or exemption from prosecution is drafted. It is then taken, together with materials in the case file, to the people's procuratorate at the same level for review and decision.

—Public and state security offices, the procuratorates and the people's courts accept complaints, accusations, and the voluntary surrender of criminals. When one of these institutions receives a criminal matter outside its jurisdiction, it must transfer such matter to one competent in handling the case and notifying the complainant. In an emergency, the receiving institution may adopt emergency measures to handle the case until such time as the transfer of the case can be made.

— A case in which a people's procuratorate has initiated public prosecution shall be submitted to the people's court for adjudication.

—When a people's court adjudicates a case initiated by the public prosecution, the people's procuratorate shall send personnel to appear in court for prosecution. In cases where the offense is relatively minor, the people's court can make an adjudication without any representation from the people's procuratorate. When the people's procuratorate protests or when a people's court of second instance demands that the people's procuratorate send personnel to appear in court, the people's procuratorate shall send personnel at the same level to appear in court.

—In cases where a criminal commits further crimes during the period in which a sentence is being served, or where criminal conduct is discovered after sentence, prisons and reform through labor institutions shall transfer the matter to the people's procuratorate for consideration. When a criminal sentenced to control, criminal detention, fixed-term imprisonment, or life imprisonment truly repents or demonstrates meritorious service during the period of his sentence, he may be granted a reduction of sentence or parole according to law. In these instances, the executing institution submits a written opinion to the people's court for consideration of the order.

— If, while administering punishment, prisons and reform through labor institutions consider a judgment to be in error, or if the criminal presents a petition, the matter shall be referred for reconsideration to the people's procuratorate or the people's court that made the original judgment.

Mutual restraint Public or state security offices, the procuratorates and the courts shall, in the light of their division of labor, supervise each other so as to guard against errors and rectify their mistakes, if any, in order to guarantee the correct implementation of the law. The way they check and balance against each other is mainly reflected in:

— A people's procuratorate may make a decision not to approve the arrest of an offender proposed by a public or state security office or to exempt from prosecution a case transferred to it for public prosecution, if the procuratorate considers that there are no sufficient grounds to make the arrest. It will deliver its decision to the public or state security office. When that office considers such a decision to be mistaken, it may demand reconsideration. If reconsideration leads to no reversal, it may request review by the people's procuratorate at the next higher level.

— In examining and approving the arrest of an offender, if a people's procuratorate discovers any illegalities in the investigation by a public or state security office, it must notify the latter to rectify them. Public or state security office should then inform the people's procuratorate of its corrections.

— In reviewing a case, if a people's procuratorate considers that re-inspection or re-examination of the investigation by a public security office is necessary, it may demand public security office to conduct a re-investigation. It may also send procuratorial personnel to participate.

— In reviewing a case in which public prosecution has been initiated by a people's procuratorate, a people's court may remand the case to the people's procuratorate for supplementary investigation, if it considers the principal facts of the crime are unclear and the evidence incomplete. Where there is no need for a criminal sentence, it may demand the people's procuratorate to withdraw prosecution. Even if the people's court has conducted public hearings on the case, it may declare the defendant innocent and release him.

—When the procuratorial personnel appearing in court discovers illegalities in the court's adjudication, he has the right to present the court with opinions on how to rectify them.

—If a people's procuratorate considers that the judgments and orders of a people's court contain actual errors, it has the right to present a protest according to appellate procedure. If the Supreme People's Procuratorate discovers actual errors in judgments and orders of the people's courts that have already been enforced, or if the people's procuratorates at higher levels discover errors in decisions by lower courts, they may protest in accordance with the procedure of adjudication supervision and exercise supervision to determine whether the adjudication activities of the people's courts were lawful.

—The people's procuratorates are to evaluate whether or not the execution of judgments or orders in criminal cases and the activities of prisons, detention houses and reform through labor institutions are lawful. If any illegalities are discovered, they shall notify the offender to rectify them.

In addition, the Criminal Procedure Law has strict and specific time provisions which must be observed by the public and state security offices, procuratorates and courts in carrying out their respective activities. The time limit urges them to apply the law in a timely and effective manner and to make earnest efforts to safeguard both the right of the prosecution and the right of the defendant. For example, Article 92 of the Criminal Procedure Law provides that the period for handling a case generally shall not exceed two months. Where the circumstances of a case are complex and the case cannot be concluded before the expiration of this period, a one-month extension may be granted with the approval of the people's procuratorate at the next level up. Article 125 of the Criminal Procedure Law stipulates that in hearing a case of public prosecution, a people's court shall announce judgment within one month after accepting the case, with no extensions beyond one and a half months.

CHAPTER 7

People's Courts

The people's courts of the People's Republic of China are judicial institutions exercising judicial power on behalf of the state. Publicly they declare that all their activities are aimed at serving the masses, at protecting the life, property, rights and interests of the people. Their duty is to hear civil and criminal cases, resolve civil disputes, punish criminals and educate citizens to conscientiously abide by the law. The purpose is to safeguard the people's democratic system and socialist legal order so that citizens can enjoy personal freedoms and democratic rights, property rights and personal well-being. The object is to facilitate the construction of a socialist civilization, both materially and spiritually.

After the founding of the People's Republic, the people's courts were established step by step according to the provisional Constitution, namely, stipulations of the Common Program of the CPPCC adopted in September 1949. In 1951, the Provisional Organic Rules of the People's Courts of the People's Republic of China was instituted. In 1954, the First NPC adopted the Organic Law of the People's Courts of the People's Republic of China which defined the nature, task and organization of the people's courts, as well as the basic principles and rules for their activities. This helped perfect China's courts at various levels.

In 1979, the Second Session of the Fifth NPC laid down a new Organic Law of the People's Courts of the People's Republic of China. This new law reiterated the former tenet that "The people's courts shall, in accordance with the law, exercise judicial power independently, and are not subject to interference by administrative institutions, public organizations or individuals," and the important principle that all citizens are equal before the law. The new law made some amendments, to wit, to the tasks of the people's courts, the system of defense, the jury system and the procedure in supervising the administration of justice. These stipulations were further affirmed by the Constitution of the People's Republic of China promulgated in 1982. In September 1983 the Second Session of the Sixth NPC Standing Committee adopted a resolution to revise the Organic Law of the People's Courts of the People's Republic of China in the light of the Constitution.

The present Constitution and the Organic Law of the People's Courts clearly define the organizational and work principles of the Chinese courts, and specifically outline the various judicial systems of the people's courts. They give guidance in handling civil and criminal cases, and provide a reference for knowing and studying the subject of courts in China.

ORGANIZATIONAL NATURE OF CHINA'S COURTS AND THEIR GUIDING PRINCIPLES

There are now more than three thousand people's courts across China. They are established to facilitate: **A.** the prompt and correct exercise of state judicial power on a national scale; **B.** the supervision over lower courts by higher courts; **C.** the participation of citizens in legal proceedings and the masses' supervision of the administration of justice; and **D.** the unification of the socialist legal system while taking into consideration the characteristics of different trades and localities.

According to the Constitution and the Organic Law of the People's Courts, the organizational system of China's courts involves "four levels and two trials." This system consists of the Supreme People's Court, local people's courts at different levels, military courts and other special people's courts. Local people's courts are divided into higher people's courts, intermediate people's courts, and primary people's courts.

The Supreme People's Court The Supreme People's Court is the highest judicial institution of the state. Its verdict or ruling on the first or second proceeding shall be final. It gives preliminary hearings to major civil and criminal cases, and any other cases it deems appropriate. For example, the Supreme People's Court set up a special court to try the Lin Biao and Jiang Qing counterrevolutionary cliques at the end of 1980.

The Supreme People's Court is also the highest body to supervise the administration of justice by the local courts at various levels, by the military courts and other special courts. According to the procedure of first appeal, it accepts and hears cases where the defendants plead not guilty and refuse to accept the verdicts or rulings brought in by a people's court of the trial level and have filed appeals to a higher court. It also reviews cases involving death sentences.

At the same time the Supreme People's Court supervises the administration of justice by people's courts at all levels and special people's courts all over China. It has the right to interpret the application of laws and decrees.

The president of the Supreme People's Court is elected by the NPC. He is responsible to, and makes a report on his work, to the NPC. His term of office is five years and no more than two consecutive terms shall be served. The NPC appoints or dismisses the deputy presidents, presiding and deputy-presiding judges, and other judges of the Supreme People's Court.

The higher people's court The higher people's court gives preliminary hearings to major civilian and criminal cases of a province, an autonomous region or a municipality directly under the Central Government. It also conducts retrials or second trials when the people's procuratorate disputes the judgment or the defendant appeals against the verdict or ruling by the intermediate people's court at the first trial level. The special people's court handles cases of a special type. The verdict or ruling brought in by the higher people's court or superior special people's court for civilian and criminal cases shall be final.

The intermediate people's court The intermediate people's court hears counterrevolutionary crimes and cases involving life imprisonment and the death penalty, as well as action against foreigners or Chinese who infringe upon the legitimate rights and interests of foreigners. It handles civil and criminal cases in an appellate capacity when the people's procuratorate disputes the judgment, or the defendant appeals against the verdict or ruling delivered by the people's court at the trial level.

The primary people's court The primary people's court means the people's court of a county, city, autonomous county or district directly under a municipality. It handles civil cases at the trial level and common criminal cases. Because China has a vast territory and a huge population, the primary people's courts may establish a number of sub-people's courts according to needs of the local area, population and circumstances of the cases to ensure timely and accurate judgment. There are now nearly ten thousand people's courts in the vast rural townships and towns of China. Court sessions of the primary people's courts bring in verdicts and rulings. The primary people's courts give guidance to the people's mediation committee.

The special people's court handles special cases in a special area. The military court is established in the People's Liberation Army to hear criminal cases involving servicemen. The railway and transport court handles criminal cases and economic disputes relating to railway and transportation. Since November 1984, marine courts (corresponding to intermediate people's courts) have been instituted in the five ports of Guangzhou, Shanghai, Qingdao, Tianjin and Dalian. They give preliminary hearings to cases involving marine business and affairs. Defendants who plead not guilty in marine courts appeal to the higher people's court of the local province or municipality.

Local people's courts at different levels organize separate tribunals for civil affairs, economic disputes and criminal cases. They may set up other tribunals when necessary. There are presiding judges and deputies for the tribunals. The presidents of the local people's courts are elected by the local people's congresses at different levels. They are responsible and report to their respective people's congresses. The standing committees of the local people's congresses appoint or dismiss the deputy presidents of the people's courts, their presiding judges and their deputies, as well as the other judges. All Chinese citizens who have reached the age of twenty-three and have the right to vote and stand for election may be elected presidents of the courts or appointed deputy presidents, presiding judges or judges, except those deprived of political rights.

All people's courts and special courts in China carry out activities according to the Constitution and Organic Law of the People's Courts. Their work relies on the following principles:

— All citizens are equal before the law regardless of nationality, race, sex, occupation, family background, religious belief, education, property status, or length of residence. No one shall have special privileges.

— The people's courts shall, in accordance with the law, exercise judicial power independently and are not subject to interference by administrative institutions, public organizations or individuals.

— All cases handled by the people's courts shall be heard in public.

— The accused has the right of defense.

— Citizens of all nationalities have the right to use the spoken and written languages of their own nationalities in court proceedings. The people's courts should provide translation for any party to court proceedings who is not familiar with the spoken or written languages in common use in the locality. In an area where people of a minority nationality live in a compact community or where a number of nationalities live together, hearings should be conducted in the language or languages in common use in the locality; indictments, judgments, notices and other documents should be written in the language or languages in common use in the locality.

The people's courts, people's procuratorates and public security offices shall, in handling criminal cases, divide their functions, each taking responsibility for its own work. They shall coordinate their efforts and check each other to ensure correct and effective enforcement of law.

BASIC JUDICIAL SYSTEM OF CHINA'S COURTS

The Constitution, the Organic Law of the People's Courts, the Criminal Procedure Law and other laws clearly prescribe the basic systems for China's courts to carry out judicial activities.

93

These systems lay the practical groundwork for fair and correct administration of justice by the courts at different levels. They ensure the promotion of socialist democracy, efficiency in handling legal cases, and safeguard the legitimate rights and interests of persons undergoing legal proceedings. The chief systems are:

Public hearings Public hearings are important for all courts in China. According to Article 125 of the Constitution, "All cases handled by the people's courts, except those involving special circumstances specified by law, shall be heard in public." This means open attendance to all who take part in the proceedings and to the public. The public prosecutor, plaintiff, defendant, agent *ad litem*, witness and appraiser are all allowed to attend court sessions where they may accuse, defend or appeal against a court decision. The general public can take seats reserved for visitors at the hearings. Newsmen are allowed to attend, obtain interviews, report on cases and publish news and comments.

"Except those involving special circumstances specified by law" means that the Organic Law of the People's Courts rules that cases involving state secrets, personal or private matters, and persons under age shall not be heard in public. This is aimed at keeping state secrets, protecting the reputation of the party to a lawsuit, securing correct statements from those not yet of age while helping them mend their ways, and avoiding the spread of bad influence to the general public. After privately hearing the cases, however, the people's courts should publicly pronounce their judgments.

Hearing cases in public, China's courts serves two purposes: The first is to put the administration of justice directly under the supervision of the public. It will help increase the sense of duty of the judicial staff and improve their style of work, resulting in stricter law enforcement and administration. Second, hearing cases in public helps publicize laws and carry on legal education among the public. In the course of open hearings, the courts spread knowledge of the legal system and encourage citizens to abide by law. Citizens in attendance receive a concrete and vivid education in law and order. This should help prevent crimes and disputes.

The system of defense Both Article 125 of the Constitution and Article 8 of the Organic Law of the People's Courts specify that "The accused has the right to defense." The accused may entrust such a right to a lawyer. Organizations such as trade unions, women's organizations or youth leagues, or the office or unit where the defendant works may recommend a citizen to act as counsel for the defendant. In addition, close relatives of the defendant and any citizen granted permission by the court may give testimony favorable to the defendant. When necessary, the court may appoint a defender for the accused. This means that the defendant can fully exercise the right to defense.

China's courts use various ways to help the accused assume the right to defense. The right to defense is an important democratic aspect in the legal proceedings of China. In the course of adjudication, the courts make efforts to help defendants exercise their right to defense and protect their legitimate rights and interests. Concurrently, this right to defense also helps the courts seek truth from facts, evaluate evidence, and mete out fair and rational sentences.

The system of recusal In any case heard by a Chinese court at any level, the person taking proceedings or the lawful agent *ad litem* has the right to ask members of the bench who are closely connected with the case to recuse themselves. The presiding judge or the president of the court should decide whether those members should be recused. This system not only safeguards the legitimate right of the person undergoing the proceedings, but prevents the judicial staff from perverting the law. It ensures a fair and correct administration of justice.

The system of a collegiate bench This is a system involving the organizational form of the court session hearing cases. There are two forms for the Chinese court—an independent bench and a collegiate bench. The independent bench consists of a single judge. The collegiate bench consists of a collective of judges or of judges and jurors. The independent bench of a single judge hears simple civil cases and minor criminal cases. Other cases are heard by the collegiate bench, which makes collective decisions on the principle of "the minority giving in to the majority." Those in the minority, however, are allowed to reserve their views. This can ensure fair and correct verdicts and rulings, and reduce errors in cases.

The system of a judicial committee The judicial committee is established in China's courts at different levels to exercise collective leadership in judicial work. Article 11 of the Organic Law of the People's Courts reads, "People's courts at all levels shall establish judicial committees to carry out democratic centralism." The task of the judicial committee is to sum up experience in judicial work and discuss vital and difficult cases as well as problems in the administration of justice. Led by the president of the court, all members of the judicial committee enjoy equal rights. If their opinions divide in a discussion, they make a decision on the principle of "the minority giving in to the majority." The collegiate bench shall execute the decision made by the judicial committee about a specific case.

The judicial committee is the product of historical experience in judicial practice in China. It plays an important part in strengthening the collective leadership of the courts and ensuring correct enforcement of state laws and decrees by the courts.

The system of verifying the death penalty China's courts keep the death sentence under strict control. To make sure that those who are sentenced to death must have committed the most heinous crimes with no alternative but to inflict capital punishment, China's courts have a system of verifying cases involving the death penalty. It is a special procedure in accordance with the related stipulations of law. It reads, "All death penalty cases shall be submitted to the Supreme People's Court for approval, except those judged by the Supreme People's Court itself. When it is necessary, the Supreme People's Court may authorize higher people's courts at the provincial, autonomous regional or municipal (directly under the Central Government) level to approve death sentences involving murder, rape, robbery, bombing, and other crimes which seriously jeopardize public security and order."

The system of supervising the administration of justice This is a special procedure in effect for re-examining wrong verdicts and rulings. If the party to a lawsuit or its relatives objects to the verdict and ruling that has taken effect, they can appeal to the court or procuratorate. Such an appeal must be seriously re-examined. If there is an erroneous verdict or ruling, it must be redressed according to the supervisory procedure. Articles 3 and 14 of the Organic Law of the People's Courts specify the procedure for correcting erroneous verdicts and rulings in effect within courts, and among superior and subordinate courts.

Adopting a supervision system to check and redress injustice embodies the high sense of responsibility China's courts have for state laws and the rights and interests of citizens. Such a system can protect against any courts committing errors, and also protect the rights and interests of the parties to a lawsuit. Whenever they are aware of, or discover, an erroneous verdict or ruling that has taken effect, China's courts must resolutely correct it. The system is diametrically opposed to such hypocritical ideas as, "No official regrets his own judgment" or "It's hard to correct a legal statement." The law rules that the supervisory procedure applies to only those cases that have taken legal effect and are indeed wrong. Such a case is submitted by the president of the court or of a superior court to the judicial committee for decision. Such cases may be re-tried. Long judicial practice by China's courts has proven that conscientiously righting erroneous verdicts and rulings in effect, and adhering to the supervision system are essential to safeguarding socialist democracy and strengthening the legal system. All China's courts uphold these systems specified by law; they are effective and are welcomed by the people.

SYSTEM FOR
CIVIL TRIALS AND PRACTICE

After they were established, China's courts instituted tribunals at all levels for hearing civil cases or disputes, and building a system of handling such cases. This system has passed through two stages of development.

The first stage came between the founding of the People's Republic in 1949 and 1976. During those years inadequate attention was paid to civil cases due to the traditional judicial habit of "Taking criminal cases seriously and civil cases lightly," and because of China's own cultural characteristics. China has long laid stress on solving the large numbers of civil disputes in daily life by the method of reconciliation between the two parties, or mediation by a third party. China's culture did not reinforce resorting to legal proceedings, court adjudication or arbitration.

Reconciliation and mediation called for the opposing parties or the mediator, under the fairest and most rational conditions possible, to devise a solution acceptable to both parties. As the system of reconciliation and mediation was popularized and applied extensively, legal procedure for civil cases remained undeveloped in China for a time. People even applied the principle of reconciliation and mediation to civil procedure. "Giving priority to mediation" became a basic principle of civil trails in China. Courts did their best to mediate a settlement in all kinds of civil disputes and to give priority to persuasion and education. They strove to avoid a court decision or arbitration needing the backing of state for enforcement. This supposedly promoted harmony and unity among the people.

As an important part of the state apparatus, however, it was evident that the court also performed the primary function of safeguarding state order with force in favor of the people. Therefore, China reconsidered the principle of "giving priority to mediation" in civil procedure. It had become apparent that as a result of unduly over-emphasizing the role of mediation to the neglect of the system of civil judgment, China had made little headway in enacting legislation for civil procedure and civil affairs in those years. Although the system of civil judgment had been established, it was far from perfect. It failed to play the role of a state regulating institution that could solve large numbers of civil disputes in the social context.

The second stage of development and perfection came after 1976. Following the overthrow of the Lin Biao and Jiang Qing counterrevolutionary cliques, China's courts began to perfect the system of civil judgment as the construction of the state legal system began. First China enacted a large number of separate statutes and laws for civil affairs and specified suitable legal standards for various concrete civil affairs, such as the marriage law, the inheritance law, the forestry law, and laws governing economic contracts, China-foreign joint ventures, environmental protection, marine environmental protection, regulations for technological transfer and for trademark. The

General Rules of Civil Law and many other separate civil statutes all have been promulgated. All this provides a legal basis for fair and rational judgment of civil cases by the people's courts. At the same time China has made efforts to enact legislation for civil procedure. It has formulated the Civil Procedure Law and temporary provisions concerning fees for civil procedure. As a result, both the court and the litigants have legal norms of conduct to abide by in the proceedings.

In addition, China has expanded its contingent of judicial personnel for handling civil cases and improved professional knowledge to meet sophisticated social relationships and the growing number of civil disputes. As state enterprises and institutions, government offices and public organizations can now be considered legal persons with corresponding rights, China has begun to institute economic tribunals in people's courts at the county level and above. They specialize in arbitrating economic disputes among state enterprises and institutions, government offices and public organizations. They have begun hearing special economic disputes such as patent rights cases.

The Civil Procedure Law of the People's Republic of China, promulgated in March 1982 for trial enforcement, defines the task, principle and procedure of the courts in trying civil cases.

Article 2 of the Civil Procedure Law and Article 3 of the Organic Law of the People's Courts stipulate that the basic task of the people's courts in handling civil affairs is to mediate and hear civil cases and to correctly apply the law to ascertain the truth and distinguish between right and wrong. They should promptly arbitrate disputes concerning title to property, economic circulation, marriage, personal freedom and other civil matters as specified by law. This will improve relations between state offices, economic organizations, enterprises, institutions and citizens, as well as relations among them. People's courts affirm the rights and duties of citizens in civil affairs, punish unlawful acts, protect the interests of the state and collective, and safeguard legitimate personal rights and interests of citizens. They educate citizens to abide by state laws conscientiously, to promote the socialist morality of maintaining discipline, to consolidate the socialist system, to uphold social and economic order, to strengthen state and social stability and unity, and to ensure the success of national socialist economic construction.

In hearing civil cases, China's courts apply general civil procedure, simple procedure, or civil procedure concerning foreign affairs according to the specific conditions of the cases. Whatever procedure they employ, they must adhere to the following basic principles and systems:

The principle of proceeding from the actual situation, seeking truth from facts, basing judgment on facts and using the law as a yardstick They should seriously carry out investigation and study, collect comprehensive evidence, acknowledge objective facts, and distinguish between right and wrong among the litigants by finding out the facts. Affirming the civil rights and duties of the parties, the courts should punish unlawful acts and protect legitimate rights and interests.

The principle that "All citizens are equal before the law" Article 5 of the Civil Procedure Law clearly specifies that law applies equally to all parties to a lawsuit. This principle requires courts to enforce law impartially in hearing civil cases, to be fair, upright, and outspoken toward all parties.

The principle of relying on the masses, making fair investigation and study, solving disputes on the spot, and placing emphasis on mediation This principle reflects a distinctive national feature most suitable to the conditions in China. China has a large population and a complex society. Civil disputes are contradictions among the people. They can be solved fairly and rationally only by following the mass line. The masses know best the real conditions of these disputes. Therefore, in the course of handling civil cases, the courts must rely on the masses and extensively conduct investigations and study. They should make efforts to mediate a settlement on the spot for the convenience of the parties. Practical experience has shown that more than seventy percent of China's civil disputes are solved through mediation. In mediating settlements, the courts must insist on the following principles:

The principle of finding out the fact and discerning between right and wrong This serves as the basis for mediation. The court should urge both parties to work in a spirit of unity and cooperation, mutual understanding and accommodation, so that they can reach an agreement resolving their disputes.

100

The principle of exercising one's own free will This means two things: **A.** The court cannot begin the mediation procedure without the free will of the parties involved. Mediation is not an absolute procedure for civil disputes, except for divorce cases. **B.** Agreement must be reached according to the free will of the parties. No side can pressure the other side to accept the agreement.

The principle of legitimacy The agreement reached through mediation must not violate state laws or policies. There shall be no unprincipled mediation.

The agreement shall take effect once it is reached. Both parties must strictly comply with its execution. If one party fails to do so, the other party can ask the court to enforce compliance.

Since they were established, the Chinese courts have solved large numbers of civil disputes. This has contributed greatly to stabilizing public economic order, defending legitimate rights of citizens, and regulating social life.

For a long time civil cases handled by the Chinese courts come under two major categories. One category consists of marriage and family disputes. The other category embraces disputes relating to property and economic rights and interests.

Marriage and family troubles account for about seventy percent of the total number of civil cases. Nonetheless, different periods of historical development have brought about changes in civil cases.

Marriage and family disputes China promulgated its first Marriage Law of the People's Republic of China in 1954. This law dismantled the old feudal system dominating marriage and family life in China for several thousand years. It has rebuilt a new socialist system of marriage and family life on the principle of freedom of marriage, one husband and one wife, equality of the sexes, protection of the legitimate rights and interests of women and their children. As a result, problems of feudal marriage and family relations left behind by old China led to a rapid growth of such lawsuits in a short time. For example, the number of marriage and family lawsuits in 1953 was more than two and a half times that in 1950. Most of them involved divorce cases of arranged marriages in feudal China, of mercenary marriages, child brides, bigamy and other forms of persecution and discrimination against women.

After 1954, the number of marriage cases fell year by year. There was a 45.7 percent decline in 1957 compared with 1953. Then in 1959 the number was down 51.98 percent from 1957. During the disastrous years of the "cultural revolution," the legal system was undermined as were the people's courts. New problems of marriage and family relations developed while large numbers of property and economic disputes were not resolved for a long time. Therefore, after the Lin Biao and Jiang Qing counterrevolutionary cliques were destroyed, and as the legal system was restored, the number of civil lawsuits grew year by year. In some places, the number of civil cases accepted by the people's courts surpassed all previous records in New China. Marriage and family disputes accounted for a high percentage, reaching two hundred percent in some places.

After revising the former marriage law, China promulgated a new marriage law in 1980. Summing up past experience, the new marriage law accounted for changes and developments in social conditions and confirmed the basic principles of socialist marriage and family relations in the original marriage law. Nonetheless, there are additional principles in the new law, protecting the legitimate rights and interests of the aged, encouraging family planning, and raising the minimum marriage age from twenty to twenty-two for men and from eighteen to twenty for women. The new law is vital to the improvement and development of a new type of socialist marriage and family relations, and to population and birth control.

Disputes over property and economic rights and interests Property disputes involve houses, inheritance, real estates, debts, compensation, forests and water conservancy facilities. Such cases are influenced by various social conditions as are marriage and family disputes. After the overthrow of the Lin Biao and Jiang Qing cliques, China published the Inheritance Law of the People's Republic of China in 1984 when it began to enforce policies resolving house property and real estate disputes. Consequently, the number of cases involving disputes over these issues rose rapidly.

Disputes about economic rights and interests involve primarily economic contracts. Most of them are controversies between corporations, or between corporations and individual businessmen. This is a new situation brought about by reforms in the economic structure and by the policy of loosening central control over the national economy. There are now many lawsuits of economic disputes, and their number is rising. The economic tribunals of the people's courts hear cases of economic disputes according to civil procedure, and are playing an increasingly important part in solving large numbers of such disputes.

CHINA'S COURTS AND THE SYSTEM OF CRIMINAL PRACTICE AND JUDGMENT

The trial of criminal cases occupies an important place in the system of judicial judgment in China. Since the establishment of a new people's court system, China has instituted criminal tribunals in courts at different levels, specializing in hearing criminal cases. It has always attached importance to criminal tribunals and provided them with an adequate judicial staff.

The hearing of criminal cases is an essential part of the judicial work of the people's courts at all levels. This is a kind of work characterized by both stern coercion and extensive democracy. Coercion embodies state judicial power exercised by the courts as state institutions of dictatorship. Democracy reflects the purpose of protecting and relying on the fulfillment of the masses' interests. The dual nature of coercion and democracy determines that China's courts should exercise state judicial power to punish all criminals who disrupt public order, and to protect the life and property of the citizens.

Through criminal procedure, the people's courts promptly and accurately ascertain the facts of various criminal activities, correctly apply law, punish criminals and protect innocent persons against criminal charges. At the same time, as the courts expose and punish criminals in the hearings, citizens learn that criminal deeds are dangerous to society. This awareness should increase the citizens' sense of observing law and fighting of criminality. This should warn those who plot treason that they must give up their intentions and become law-abiding citizens.

As a result, crime will be reduced, and the socialist political system and economic base will be consolidated. In this way people's courts uphold the socialist legal system and protect the individual freedoms of citizens, as well as other legitimate rights.

In hearing criminal cases, China's courts strictly observe both substantive and procedural law. China's criminal legislation is quite complete, providing sufficient grounds for the courts to try criminal cases. The Criminal Law of the People's Republic of China and the Criminal Procedure Law of the People's Republic of China were published in July 1979, and enforced in January 1980. In addition, there are large numbers of separate criminal laws and regulations. According to the related stipulations of China's criminal legislation, the people's courts must adhere to the following principles in the course of hearing criminal cases:

Hearing cases independently and submitting to law only This is the fundamental principle of China's courts, which is particularly underlined in trying criminal cases. In hearing criminal cases, the courts must strictly base their work on facts and employ law as a criterion. They are not to be subject to interference or influence by any administrative offices, public organizations or individuals.

The principle of combining punishment with leniency In meting out punishment, the courts take into account subjective and objective conditions and try to win over and reform the great majority of criminals while isolating and punishing the minority.

They deal with different types of criminals in different ways, coupling penalties with leniency. For instance, they punish primary culprits severely and accessories lightly. Those who have been coerced to commit crimes or inveigled into doing so receive light penalties or no penalty at all. Recidivists and habitual criminals are punished severely. Accidental offenders are punished lightly. Severe penalties are imposed on those who refuse to confess their crimes. Those who surrender themselves and perform meritorious service are treated leniently. Criminals caught in the act shall be dealt with seriously, while those, who committed past crimes and have lived peacefully since these transgressions, shall be punished leniently. Those who involve children in crime shall be punished severely, while juvenile criminals shall be treated leniently.

The principle of combining punishment with education This is a fundamental characteristic of China's criminal legislation and judicature. The courts carry out a policy of combining ideological education with productive labor for criminals who have been sentenced, laying stress on ideological reform. They aim at transforming these criminals into new persons who can live on their own toil without doing harm to the public.

The Criminal Law of the People's Republic of China lists five kinds of major penalties and three additional penalties for criminals. The five major penalties are "surveillance," "detention in custody," "a term of imprisonment," "life imprisonment" and " death." The three additional penalties are fine of money, deprivation of political rights and confiscation of property. They may be inflicted independently.

Criminals who have committed minor crimes doing little harm to the public shall not be put in prison, but shall return to the public while being put under the surveillance of the government and supervision of the masses. Their personal rights shall be restricted to a certain extent, and they must accept ideological education to reform themselves. The minimum term of the " surveillance penalty" is three months and the maximum term two years. During this term, criminals can live with their families and continue to work at their former jobs, enjoying equal pay for equal work. This penalty embodies China's policy of imprisoning as few criminals as possible, and is instrumental in reforming minor criminals. It is an effective method of punishment.

China's courts lay emphasis on imposing very few death penalties. Some criminals have committed abominable crimes with serious consequences to the public and should be sentenced to death according to criminal law. Nonetheless, provided they are not guilty of the most heinous crimes involving murder, they shall not receive the death penalty. Only those, who have perpetrated the gravest crimes in the most evil way causing great harm to the public, therefore arousing utmost popular indignation, will be sentenced to death. Some, however, will be sentenced to death with a two-year stay of the execution of sentence. During this two-year period, these offenders are given a last opportunity to repent and mend their ways by reform through labor. The death penalty with the two—year stay of the execution of sentence demonstrates a policy of revolutionary humanitarianism striving to execute as few criminals as possible, focusing, instead, on an effective way to transform them back into useful members of society.

The policy of revolutionary humanitarianism toward convicted criminals This policy provides all criminals, except those sentenced to death, with the opportunity to earn a living. The government carries out a policy of combining ideological education and productive labor for all convicted criminals, whether they serve their sentences in prisons, in workshops, or on farms to reform themselves through labor. This is aimed at transforming them into new persons of value to the public. To encourage criminals to correct their errors and make a fresh start, the courts have instituted a series of penalty systems including reprieve, commutation and release on parole. This sparks hope for a new life among most criminals and increases their faith in reforming themselves. As a result, the great majority of criminals have the opportunity to mend their ways and work for the public good. Many have mastered a special skill working for society during their term of labor. China's system of criminal judgment has transformed many Chinese and Japanese war criminals. It has even turned the last emperor of the Qing Dynasty, Puyi, into a new man earning his own living.

The policy of applying legal principles with flexibility This policy is shown in the following aspects:

Adapting the criminal law to localities The criminal law is a fundamental law universally effective on a national scale. In national autonomous regions, however, institutions of state power at the autonomous regional, or provincial, level could make adaptations or supplementary regulations according to the local political, economic and cultural characteristics, and to basic principles of the criminal law.

Adherence to lawful classification of crimes while allowing for designations by analogy on a strictly limited basis Detailed regulations of the criminal law specify about two hundred crimes. It is a fundamental principle to convict criminals who have violated these laws according to a unified criterion. It also is permissible to designate crimes not included in the detailed regulations of the criminal law by referring to similar crimes. But this must be reported to the Supreme People's Court for approval.

Range of penalties Penalties are prescribed within a certain range so that the judicial staff may exercise discretion in imposing a severe or light penalty according to specifics of the case.

The principle of basing judgments on facts and applying law as the criterion In sentencing a criminal, the court must proceed from actual conditions, make an investigation, and seek truth from facts. It must rely on evidence and not readily believe in confessions.

Correcting any mistakes constitutes an important part of this principle. To ensure the correction of errors, both defendants or procuratorates are allowed to object to court decisions and appeal to higher courts in the course of adjudication. They may do so after the court decisions, believed to be in error, have taken legal effect. Such errors must be corrected according to the supervision procedure. For instance, in the two years between May 1978 and June 1980, China's courts at different levels re-examined a total of 1.2 million criminal cases judged during the "cultural revolution," and corrected 251,000 erroneous or false cases involving 267,000 persons. As a result, large numbers of persons who had been persecuted by the Lin Biao and Jiang Qing cliques had their cases redressed and their good names restored. This also restored and strengthened the righteousness of the state legal system.

Although the system of criminal judgment plays a great part in reducing and preventing crimes in China, criminal acts continue to take place as a social phenomenon. Despite the fact that socialism has taken root in China, China is poor and backward compared with developed countries. Vestiges of the old semi-feudal, semi-colonial China still exist along with the force of traditional habits, providing a breeding ground for crimes.

In the early years after the founding of the People's Republic, criminality abounded. There were, roughly, nine counter-revolutionary or other criminals for every ten thousand of the total population. Thanks to the efforts of the judicial institutions, the criminal rate fell year by year. On the eve of the "cultural revolution," the ratio of the number of criminals to the total population dropped to three per ten thousand. During the years of the "cultural revolution," however, China's judiciary was destroyed and its legal system damaged. The proportion of crimes once again began to rise and approached seven per ten thousand in 1979.

During the "cultural revolution," anarchism spread unchecked. The masses were engaged in armed conflicts everywhere adversely influencing the young generation. As a result, juvenile delinquency is quite conspicuous today. There are large numbers of crimes involving murder, rape, plunder, theft, corruption, smuggling, speculation and profiteering, disturbance of public order, and hooliganism. It is the primary task of the courts to suppress this type of behavior.

Apart from strengthening judicial work against criminal activities, China is taking various measures to publicize laws and information concerning the legal system among the public. This is regarded as a comprehensive treatment to reduce crime by involving the whole of society. Teen-agers who have committed grave crimes and have left serious consequences for the public, must be punished according to law. Others who are generally not charged with criminal action, instead, are educated and reformed in disciplinary institutes or work-study schools for juvenile delinquents run by state administrative institutions. There, they learn to read and write, study law, and do manual labor. Through the education of study and labor, the state tries to transform as many juvenile delinquents as possible. For instance, China's courts charged only 18.9 percent of the total number of juvenile delinquents with criminal action in 1980. Closely coordinated with criminal adjudication by the courts, the comprehensive treatment project is an important part of reducing and preventing crimes.

CHAPTER 8

People's Procuratorates

China's procuratorates are state institutions responsible for supervision of law enforcement. They safeguard the people's democracy and guarantee the smooth progression of the drive for socialist modernization. They generally exercise supervision over counterrevolutionary cases and other forms of criminality. Their official title is the people's procuratorates of the People's Republic of China, known in short as the people's procuratorates. As their name suggests, they represent the will of the people and are aimed at safeguarding the people's democratic system and serving the interests of the people.

After the founding of the People's Republic, China began to set up its Supreme People's Procuratorial Office and started work for establishing local procuratorates at different levels. In September 1951, the Central People's Government adopted the Provisional Organic Regulations of the Supreme People's Procuratorial Office and the General Organic Rules of the Local Procuratorial Offices at Different Levels. In September 1954, the First NPC adopted at its First Session the Organic Law of the Supreme People's Procuratorate of the People's Republic of China changing the people's procuratorial offices into the people's procuratorates. Specific provisions for the functions and powers of the people's procuratorates, principles guiding its organic structure and activities, and procedure for exercising its functions and powers were made. This resulted in the gradual establishment and steady improvement of the people's procuratorates at various levels. After 1975, however, the people's procuratorates were abolished for a time, with the public security offices exercising their functions and powers.

Then in March 1978, the Fifth NPC decided at its First Session to rebuild the people's procuratorates. The Second Session revised and released in July 1979 the Organic Law of the People's Procuratorates of the People's Republic of China. In September 1983, the Sixth NPC Standing Committee adopted at its Second Session the Decision on the Revision of the Organic Law of the People's Procuratorates of the People's Republic of China. Consisting of three chapters and twenty-eight articles, the revised organic law specified systematically the nature, tasks, functions and powers of China's procuratorates, the procedure for exercising their functions and powers, their organic structure and the appointment and dismissal of their personnel.

The Organic Law of the People's Procuratorates is a basic legal document for understanding and studying China's procuratorates and its procuratorial system.

TASKS, FUNCTIONS AND POWERS

To guarantee the enforcement of China's laws and regulations, the working class and the masses exercise various forms of supervision. One of them is state supervision carried out by the NPC and its Standing Committee. The local people's congresses at different levels and their standing committees exercise supervision over the implementation of the Constitution, state laws, decrees, and regulations in their respective localities. Another form of supervision is that exercised by the state administrative institutions. They supervise activities of all their subordinate departments and enterprises, and enforcement of laws, decrees, and government resolutions. The third form of supervision is social supervision, i.e., supervision over law enforcement exercised by the people, and such popular organizations as trade unions and women's federations. State supervision is carried out from top to bottom whereas social supervision goes from bottom to top. When integrated, they form a complete supervision.

In addition to the above-mentioned forms of supervision, China has instituted people's procuratorates which serve as special institutions for supervision over law enforcement. Article 1 of the Organic Law of the People's Procuratorates of the People's Republic of China provides that people's procuratorates are state institutions responsible for supervision over the enforcement of law. They guarantee the unified implementation of laws and decrees by using procuratorial power exercised by people's procuratorates. In China criminal activities still exist: There are spies and special agents, criminal elements intent on disrupting social order, embezzlers, and profiteers.

Criminal activities within society will continue unabated for a fairly long period of time. To struggle against them, it is imperative to enact laws and regulations that can control criminality, and administer due punishment to offenders. Special institutions are a must for the supervision of the correct enforcement of law. During the "culture revolution," the Lin Biao and Jiang Qing counterrevolutionary cliques seriously sabotaged the socialist legal system and democracy. This bitter lesson tells us that we must have special institutions to oversee law enforcement. It is precisely this lesson that caused China to rebuild its people's procuratorates in 1978.

As specified in the Organic Law of the People's Procuratorates of the People's Republic of China, the tasks of the people's procuratorates are suppression of all activities aimed at betraying the state, striking heavy blows at counterrevolutionaries and other criminal elements, safeguarding the unification of the country, the system of the people's democratic dictatorship, and the socialist legal system. Therefore, the people's procuratorates maintain social order, to wit, order in production, work, education, scientific research, and in people's lives. They protect socialist property owned by the people, property owned collectively by the workers, and legally owned private property. They also protect the rights of citizens, democratic rights and other rights, and safeguard the smooth drive for socialist modernization. In addition, by exposing and prosecuting the criminal activities of the counterrevolutionaries and other criminal elements, the people's procuratorates help educate the people to be loyal to the motherland, to conscientiously observe the Constitution and other laws, to enhance the people's awareness of the law, and to actively struggle against offenders of the law.

In the light of the functions and powers as designated in the Organic Law of the People's Procuratorates, the people's procuratorates of different levels exercise the following supervision of law enforcement:

Supervision of law and discipline This is a direct struggle waged by the people's procuratorates against the offenders of the law. The first paragraph in Article 5 of the Organic Law of the People's Procuratorates stipulates that "Procuratorial power shall be exercised against criminal cases involving national security, and against the criminal disruption of a unified implementation of state policies, laws, decrees, and orders."

This is an extremely important function with which the procuratorates are charged by the state. China's actual situation shows that some people exploit their positions and powers to disrupt the unification of the country, split national unity, and endanger political power based on the Chinese people's democratic dictatorship and socialist system. Most outstanding of these types of criminal cases are cases of counterrevolution. They must be investigated by the people's procuratorates on behalf of the state and submitted to judicial institutions for severe punishment, so as to safeguard national unification and the people's democratic dictatorship. This constitutes the major and most important task for China's procuratorates in its supervision of law and discipline. The administration of law and discipline also includes supervision of state institutions and their personnel to see if the Constitution and other laws are observed. Procuratorial power is exercised whenever there are legal violations. Cases of encroaching upon citizens' democratic rights and of dereliction of duty shall be directly accepted, filed, and investigated by the people's procuratorates.

After investigation, the people's procuratorates shall initiate public prosecution in the people's courts. Cases of this type generally involve criminal acts of encroaching on the legal rights of citizens and instances of a serious dereliction of duty, resulting in grave damage to the interests of the state and its citizens. According to provisions of the Criminal Procedure Law and other relevant laws, there are fourteen kinds of criminal cases that fall under law and discipline supervision, and should be accepted directly by the people's procuratorates: extorting confessions during interrogation; bringing false charges; disrupting elections; illegal detention; illegal searches; taking reprisals and false accusations; illegal deprivation of the freedom of religious beliefs; bringing accusations with false evidence; concealing criminal evidence; encroaching upon freedom of communications; disclosing state secrets; unlawful investigation and judgment; unlawful release of criminals; and unauthorized opening, concealing, and destroying of postal mails and telegrams. In addition, there are other cases which are necessary for the procuratorates to handle directly. They are criminal acts chiefly committed by state institutions and their working personnel, but some crimes, such as disruption of election, are not necessarily perpetrated by state personnel.

Economic supervision An important task of the people's procuratorates in the direct service of socialist economic construction, economic supervision is the exercise of procuratorial power to fight against crimes in the economic sphere. Such supervision serves to guarantee the implementation of state economic policies, laws and decrees, and the maintenance of the socialist economic order. Economic supervision protects property owned by the people, property collectively owned by workers, and lawfully owned private property. In the area of production, economic supervision leads to advancement in scientific management in various sectors of the national economy and encourages the handling of economic matters according to law.

At present, there are many criminal acts in the economic sphere and some are rather serious. Cases of dereliction of duty or negligence often cause death and injuries, resulting in heavy economic losses. For instance, the No. 2 Drilling Platform of the Tianjin Offshore Oil Prospecting Bureau under the Ministry of Oil capsized in Bohai Sea due to negligence. The accident caused the death of seventy-two people, and direct economic loss of some thirty-seven million yuan. Embezzlement of a large amount of state funds in Heilongjiang Province by a gang headed by Wang Shouxing, manager of the Binxian County Fuels Company, resulted in the loss of over half a million yuan. Therefore, strengthening economic supervision is imperative for China's economic construction. At present, the following forms

113

of economic corruption should be handled directly by the people's procuratorates: offering or accepting bribes; smuggling and profiteering; destructive lumbering; causing major accidents due to negligence or dereliction of duty; counterfeiting trademarks; misappropriating funds or materials for disaster relief; evading or refusing to pay tax; and other economic crimes the people's procuratorates consider necessary to handle directly.

Criminal case supervision The people's procuratorates exercise procuratorial power against cases of counterrevolution and general criminal cases to protect the people, to maintain social order, and to safeguard the socialist legal system. They appear in court to support public prosecution, examine criminal cases endangering social order, and decide whether or not to approve the arrest and prosecution of offenders.

The people's procuratorates examine the cases investigated by public security institutions and decide whether to arrest the offender and initiate prosecutions. According to provisions of the Constitution and the Criminal Procedure Law, except for certain special circumstances in which a people's court may decide to arrest an offender, only the people's procuratorates have the right to approve the arrest of an offender. People's procuratorates also examine cases investigated and concluded by public security institutions. When procuratorial personnel discover illegalities in investigations, they should present their oral or written opinions on how to rectify them.

The procuratorates shall initiate public prosecution against criminal cases, support public prosecution, and exercise supervision to determine whether the judicial activities of people's courts are lawful. In China, procuratorates serve as state prosecution institutions. On behalf of the state, they initiate public prosecutions in the courts and subject the defendant to adjudication. When a court holds public hearings, procuratorial personnel will appear in court in the capacity of state prosecutors. The procuratorates also determine whether adjudication procedure, including the composition of adjudication personnel, and the exercise of the defendant's procedural rights, are lawful. If procuratorial personnel discover illegalities, they shall present the tribunal with opinions on how to rectify them. The

114

procuratorates supervise the judgment and orders of the courts so as to guarantee correct enforcement of the law.

Supervision over prisons, detention houses and reforms through labor institutions Provisions in the fifth paragraph of Article 5 of the Organic Law of the People's Procuratorates and Article 164 of the Criminal Procedure Law govern this area. Article 164 stipulates that "The people's procuratorates are to exercise supervision to determine whether or not the execution of judgments or orders in criminal cases and the activities of prisons, detention houses and reform through labor institutions are lawful. If they discover any illegalities, they shall notify the executing body to rectify them." The supervision over prisons, detention houses, and reform through labor farms must coordinate with prisons and reform through labor institutions so as to enable offenders to undergo reform through labor. On November 29, 1979, the Fifth NPC Standing Committee approved at its Twelfth Session the Supplementary Regulations of the State Council on Reform Through Labor. Article 5 of the supplementary regulations provide that "The people's procuratorates exercise supervision over the activities of the reform through labor institutions."

In China, reformation of offenders extends beyond mere imprisonment to enable them to reform by transforming destructive traits into beneficial ones, so as to eliminate their criminal characteristics. Reform through labor institutions are established so that offenders can go through the process of reform and become useful again to society. The people's procuratorates are given full scope in law enforcement supervision so they can use their authority to urge offenders to accept reform. In cases where criminals undergoing reform commit new crimes, their cases should be filed and investigated, and due punishment meted out.

ORGANIZATIONS

According to the Constitution and the Organic Law of the People's Procuratorates, China establishes the Supreme People's Procuratorate and the local people's procuratorates at different levels, military procuratorates and other special people's procuratorates.

The Supreme People's Procuratorate is the highest procuratorial body. Public prosecutions shall be filed at the Supreme People's Procuratorate for major criminal cases. If the Supreme People's Procuratorate uncovers errors in judgments and orders of the people's courts at different levels which have become legally effective, it has the right to present a protest in accordance with the procedure of adjudication supervision. The Supreme People's Procuratorate directs the work of the local people's procuratorates at different levels, and of the special people's procuratorates, with the right of supervision over their work and personnel staffing.

Local people's procuratorates include:

—People's procuratorates of the provinces, autonomous regions and municipalities directly under the Central Government;

—Branches of people's procuratorates of the provinces, autonomous regions and municipalities directly under the Central Government; and people's procuratorates of autonomous prefectures and cities directly under the provincial government; and

— People's procuratorates of the counties, cities, autonomous counties and districts under the jurisdiction of the cities.

People's procuratorates at the provincial and county levels may, in view of actual needs and upon the approval of the standing committee of the people's congress at the corresponding level, establish people's procuratorates at mining areas, land reclamation areas and forestry areas to serve as their procuratorial agencies. The establishment of such agencies is designed to meet the needs of China's booming economic construction. In some economic areas, many factories, mines, farm and forestry enterprises have been set up. Cases in these areas need corresponding judicial institutions in order to safeguard the legitimate rights and interests of the workers and other employees. As political powers have not been established in these economic areas, they have no people's congress of a corresponding level, so procurators-general and procurators cannot be elected or appointed by a people's congress. Therefore, the Organic Law of the People's Procuratorates provides that the people's

116

procuratorates at the provincial and county levels submit a proposal to the standing committee of the people's congress at the corresponding level for approval of the establishment of such agencies in those economic areas. In areas where there are agencies of people's procuratorates, there should be public security institutions and people's courts as well, so that they can handle criminal cases according to the legal procedure.

Special people's procuratorates are procuratorial institutions established in certain organizations. Including military procuratorates and railway and transport procuratorates, the special procuratorates operate under the guidance of the special procuratorates at higher levels and the Supreme People's Procuratorate.

Personnel of the people's procuratorates at different levels consist of a procurator-general, a deputy procurator-general, and a number of procurators, assistant procurators, and clerks. In addition, the procuratorates have a staff engaging in the study of law, carrying out clerical work, and conducting administrative affairs.

There are procuratorial committees under the people's procuratorates at different levels. The second paragraph of Article 3 of the Organic Law of the People's Procuratorates stipulates: "The people's procuratorates at different levels establish procuratorial committees. Under the auspices of the procurator-general, the committee discusses and makes decisions on major cases and important issues."

Members of the procuratorial committees are appointed according to procedure of law and consist of a procurator-general, a deputy procurator-general, some of the procurators and other personnel. The committee members primarily are involved in difficult cases and those with political significance. They determine ways to implement state principles, policies, and standing committee resolutions, summarize procuratorial experience, and work out rules and regulations concerning procuratorial work. Decisions of the procuratorial committees on important issues are executed in the name of the procuratorate or of the procurator-general. Procuratorial committees are internal institutions of power within the procuratorate. They do not handle daily routine work of the

117

procuratorates.

Organizationally, Article 20 of the Organic Law of the People's Procuratorates provides that "The Supreme People's Procuratorate establishes a criminal case department, a law enforcement department, a department supervising prisons and other correctional facilities, and an economic supervision department. It may also establish other departments in the light of specific conditions." The establishment of the people's procuratorates at different levels is basically the same as that of the Supreme People's Procuratorate. Procuratorial departments are responsible for examining and approving proposals for arrest of an offender in those criminal cases transferred by a public security institution, examining and instituting public prosecutions, and appearing in public court hearings. The law enforcement department is responsible for handling criminal violations of law and discipline by state personnel and cadres at grassroots levels. The economic supervision department is responsible for handling cases of economic crimes falling under the jurisdiction of this department. The department in charge of prisons, detention houses and reform through labor institutions is responsible for exercising procuratorial and supervisory work over prisons, detention houses, and reform through labor institutions. To maintain close contact with the people and accept their accusations and appeals, people's procuratorates at different levels also have correspondence and reception departments to respond to letters and receive visitors.

The procurator-general of the Supreme People's Procuratorate is elected and dismissed from office by the NPC. The term of office is five years and shall be served for no more than two consecutive terms. Procurators-general of the people's procuratorates of provinces, autonomous regions, and municipalities directly under the Central Government are elected and dismissed from office by the people's congresses at their corresponding levels. Their appointment or dismissal from office shall be submitted to the procurator-general of the Supreme People's Procuratorate and then to the NPC Standing Committee for approval. The procurators-general of the people's procuratorates of the autonomous prefectures, cities directly under the provincial government, counties, autonomous counties, cities and municipal districts are elected and dismissed from office by the people's congress at their corresponding levels. Their appointment or dismissal shall be submitted to the procurators-general of the procuratorates at higher levels, and then to the standing committees of the people's congresses at higher levels for approval. The term of office of the procurators-general is the same as that of the various people's congresses. The standing committees of the people's congresses at the national level and of the provinces, autonomous regions, and municipalities directly under the Central Government may, upon the proposal of the procurators-general at the corresponding level, dismiss and replace the procurators-general of the procuratorates at lower levels and their deputy procurators-general along with members of procuratorial committees.

Organizationally, the people's procuratorates are based on dual leadership and the principle of democratic centralism. They differ from the practice of vertical leadership and the individual responsibility system. According to the 1982 Constitution and the Organic Law of the People's Procuratorates, local people's procuratorates at different levels are at once subject to the leadership of the institutions of state power at the parallel level, and to the leadership of the people's procuratorates at higher levels. The exercise of unified procuratorial power by the people's procuratorates throughout the country is thus ensured.

The people's procuratorates accept the leadership of the institutions of state power at parallel level. This is demonstrated in a number of ways. The people's procuratorates report on their work to the people's congresses and their standing committees. The people's congresses and their standing committees then examine and approve the reports of the people's procuratorates at their levels. The procurators-general of the people's procuratorates at various levels are elected and dismissed from office by their people's congresses. The deputy procurators-general, procuratorial committee members, and procurators are appointed and dismissed from office by the standing committees of the people's congresses at their levels upon the nomination of the procurators-general. The appointment and dismissal of the procurators-general at different local levels are submitted to higher procurators-general, and then to the standing committees of the people's congresses at even higher levels for approval. The standing committees of people's congresses have the right to examine the work of their people's procuratorates, to reply officially to disputes among procuratorial committee members submitted by procurators-general, and to approve establishment of procuratorial agencies of the people's procuratorates.

The principle of democratic centralism practiced by the people's procuratorates is demonstrated by the fact that all the people's procuratorates practice collective leadership by procuratorial committees, and decisions on major cases or problems are shaped by the principle that the minority is subordinate to the majority. Should the procurator-general disagree with the opinion of the majority, however, he may submit the decision to the standing committee for review.

PRINCIPLES

Article 7 of the Organic Law of the People's Procuratorates provides that " The people's procuratorates seek truth from facts, pursue the mass line, heed the voice of the people, put themselves under the supervision of the people, make investigations and study, put emphasis on evidence, not readily give credence to oral statements, prohibit obtaining confessions by compulsion, and distinguish contradictions between the enemy and the people from those among the people, and manage them correctly." This provision of the organic law embodies the fine tradition fostered by the years of work of the people's procuratorates, which have been institutionalized into written form. The essence of this fine tradition lies in seeking truth from facts and following the mass line. Seeking truth from facts means taking scientific approaches, and following the mass line means pursuing the people's democratic principles.

The work principles of the people's procuratorates in accordance with the above guidelines and relevant provisions of the Criminal Procedure Law are: lawful and independent exercise of procuratorial power; equality before the law; seeking truth from facts by investigation and study with the law as the ultimate criterion; separation of responsibilities; and handling criminal cases accurately and expeditiously. These work principles must be consistent with the mass line. Closely integrated, they seek to guarantee proper development and proper functioning of the people's procuratorates.

Lawful exercise of procuratorial power Article 9 of the Organic Law of the People's Procuratorates stipulates: " The people's procuratorates shall exercise procuratorial power independently according to provisions of the law and are not subject to interference by administrative institutions, public organizations, or individuals." The people's procuratorates must exercise procuratorial power as provided by the Constitution and the Organic Law of the People's Procuratorates. This applies in the functioning of the people's procuratorates as well as the procedures they are required to follow. If the people's procuratorates abuse their powers or fail to function, they will be investigated.

In exercising procuratorial power according to the Criminal Law and other relevant laws and regulations, the people's procuratorates should strictly distinguish " guilty" from " not guilty." They should earnestly implement the Criminal Procedure Law and other procedural laws to expose crimes effectively. Also, the people's procuratorates should be scrupulous in their relationship with other institutions of state power. This principle of independence guarantees the right of the people's procuratorates to exercise procuratorial power on behalf of the state, a right granted only to the people's procuratorates by the people.

The independent exercise of procuratorial power by the people's procuratorates in China is different from the judicial independence of the Western countries. In China, the NPC and its Standing Committee are unified institutions of state power, and procuratorial power is part of state power. Article 10 of the Organic Law of the People's Procuratorates provides that "The Supreme People's Procuratorate is responsible, and reports its work, to the NPC and its Standing Committee. Local people's procuratorates at different levels are responsible, and report their work, to their people's congresses and their standing committees." Essentially, the people's procuratorates are responsible to their people's congresses and they should listen to, and accept, the supervision of the people.

121

Equality before the law Article 8 of the Organic Law of the People's Procuratorates and relevant articles of the Criminal Procedure Law stipulate that people's procuratorates, when exercising procuratorial power, shall treat all citizens as equal before the law. Equality before the law is an essential part of the democratic spirit of the socialist legal system. This principle requires the people's procuratorates in handling cases to treat all citizens as equal, regardless of their nationality, race, sex, occupation, social backgrounds, religious beliefs, educational level, property, or duration of residence. This principle protects the legal rights and interests of all citizens, including those of criminal defendants. Yet all offenders, regardless of their social status or family backgrounds, shall also be treated according to the law. Those who should be investigated will be prosecuted and adjudicated by the people's court. If the acts of a defendant are not serious enough to be judged as crimes, he should be declared innocent, no matter who he is. This principle safeguards the dignity of the law and prevents anyone from rising above the law. China does not recognize privileges. Recognition of privileges is feudal.

In China, all legal offenders, regardless of position, are subject to criminal investigation and are punished according to law. In China, feudalism had existed for several thousand years. China is still a developing country and its culture and economy have yet to modernize uniformly. In treating all citizens as equal before the law, the people's procuratorates have much work before them. Only by accomplishing it can they uphold the socialist legal system and the principle of equality before the law.

Accuracy and timeliness Accuracy means clarification of the nature of crimes so that the facts of cases are clear and the evidence reliable. Only on this basis can people's procuratorates apply the law correctly and handle cases in an accurate and timely manner. To clarify the facts of the cases, it is necessary to answer the following questions: **A.** Who was the perpetrator of the criminal act? **B.** Where exactly did the criminal act take place? **C.** What was the nature of the criminal act? **D.** Why was the act perpetrated? **E.** By what means was the crime accomplished? **F.** How was the crime perpetrated? **G.** If a crime was jointly committed, what was the relationship between the criminals?

Apart from clarifying these basic facts, people's

122

procuratorates must apply the laws and decrees correctly, so as to determine whether a crime occurred, and if so, mete out punishment accurately. China's procuratorates should handle criminal cases not only accurately but in a timely fashion. The Criminal Procedure Law has specific provisions for time limits for investigation, detention and initiation of public prosecutions. The law also requires people's procuratorates to carry out the investigation, examine and approve any proposal for the arrest of offenders, examine the cases and initiate public prosecutions, all in an expeditious manner. The speed of the investigation should, however, be determined by the necessity for acquiring all the basic facts of the case. China's procuratorates object to the erroneous notion of rapidity at the expense of thoroughness, accuracy and impartiality. For cases to be handled according to the law, all the facts surrounding the criminal act must be clarified and ascertained.

CHAPTER *9*

Public and State Security Institutions

Public and state security institutions perform the important functions of political and legal security work in China's system of administrative organizations. They are an armed administrative force charged with maintaining public order and the security of the state. The large amount of work they carry on is vital to maintaining social and production order in both city and country. They protect citizens and their property, ensure success in economic construction and activities, and maintain the security and stability of the state.

ESTABLISHMENT OF PUBLIC SECURITY INSTITUTIONS

The Ministry of Public Security is the armed administrative force charged with keeping public order in the country. Its institutions are important tools for upholding the political power of the people's democratic dictatorship. China's public security institutions are development of the Special Service Section in the First Revolutionary Civil War (1919-1927). With a relatively long history, they accumulated rich experiences in security work. During the Second Revolutionary Civil War, the Anti-Japanese War and the War of Liberation that heralded the birth of the People's Republic, public security institutions played a key role in areas where the regular armed forces were not successful. They contributed greatly to the safety of revolutionary base areas, to maintaining public order, ferreting out the hidden enemy,

124

recruiting new soldiers, and providing security behind the lines. They helped achieve the final victory of the Chinese revolution and found the People's Republic of China.

After the founding of the People's Republic in 1949, the work of public security grew and developed. Public security offices were instituted and relevant legislation was enacted. Gradually, China's public security institutions became systematized and legalized.

Today, the Ministry of Public Security under the State Council exercises unified leadership over all public security organizations in China. It was established as soon as the People's Republic was founded. The State Council has authorized it to organize and direct public security work across the country, and maintain communication and cooperation with international police organizations. Besides giving administrative and professional guidance to public security institutions at lower levels, the Ministry of Public Security studies the technology and policies of public security and develops rules and regulations to promote public security legislation. The ministry is led by, and reports to, the State Council.

There are public security departments in provinces and autonomous regions, and public security bureaus in municipalities directly under the Central Government. They are responsible for organizing and directing public security work in their respective areas. Since all of the provinces, autonomous regions and municipalities directly under the Central Government control vast administrative areas with big populations each comparing to a medium-sized country abroad, the work of maintaining public order is very complicated. Hence, it is essential to establish public security departments and bureaus concentrating their work on directing and coordinating subordinate public security institutions in various places. They study public security technology and policies, make investigations to keep abreast of the current state of the public order situation, and try to maintain public order.

Public security institutions in the provinces, autonomous regions and municipalities directly under the Central Government are led by both the Ministry of Public Security and the people's governments at the respective levels. The Ministry of

Public Security gives guidance in technology and policies to the people's governments in administration. The public security departments in provinces, autonomous regions and municipalities directly under the Central Government could establish public security sections or bureaus in areas under prefectural administrative offices which are authorized to organize and direct public security work in the rural areas under their jurisdiction.

Public security bureaus are universally established in autonomous prefectures, counties, autonomous counties and banners (an administrative division of county level in the Inner Mongolia Autonomous Region), and public security sub-bureaus in urban districts. They are China's grassroots public security institutions. Responsible for keeping public order, they are essential to China's public security system.

The public security bureaus everywhere in China establish police stations, police sub-stations, or special commissions as their agencies. These agencies are in charge of census registration, management of special trades, maintaining public order, and control of criminal activities.

Public security institutions are also instituted in railway, communications, and forestry departments. Large industrial plants and mines have also established public security departments. Mass public self-managing security organizations have also been established under the guidance of grassroots public security institutions. All form a comprehensive, well-coordinated public security system in China.

To maintain public order, public security institutions have established special professional systems, such as criminal affairs police, census registration police, public order police, traffic police, foreign affairs police, anti-explosive police, fire-brigade police and armed police.

The police are divided into two categories, professional and obligatory. Most of those working in public security are professional cadres or professional police. Only some special police, such as fire-brigade police and armed police, are obligatory police, such as soldiers performing compulsory military service in the armed forces.

As the role of public security develops, its varied organizational structure is continually reformed and perfected.

In the early years of the 1950s, the primary task of public security institutions was to consolidate the newly-born political power of the state. Two things needed to be accomplished. First, the problems left by history had to be solved; for example, punishing counterrevolutionaries and criminals, prohibiting the sale and consumption of drugs, and eradicating prostitution. After initial success in these areas, public security began to focus its attention on maintaining public order, controlling crime, and strengthening the administration of public security work. To meet their objective, they emphasized establishing an armed force to control public order, resulting in the establishment of a police service.

As the focus of national work shifted to socialist economic construction, the function of public security again underwent change. The focus of public security work shifted from crime control and prevention to ensuring traffic safety in cities and towns, and to fire control. The state law clearly defined the task of public security institutions as combating all counter-revolutionary and criminal activities, preventing and suppressing sabotage by criminals, keeping public order, protecting socialist public property, safeguarding citizens' legitimate rights and interests, defending the people's democratic dictatorship and the state, and ensuring the successful construction of socialist modernization. The change in these tasks has promoted the building of public security institutions and perfected the establishment of police services.

As China carries out a policy of opening to the outside world and increasing international political, cultural, and economic exchanges, public security institutions assume even heavier burdens. They must guard against international spies and terrorists, strengthen their control of public order, and be even more effective in their control and prevention of crime. As a result, the State Council and the Central Military Commission decided in 1983 to establish a people's armed police force and a state security office. Part of the tasks of the public security institutions were transferred to the people's armed police force, state security institutions, and respective judicial departments. Consequently, public security institutions can concentrate on maintaining public order.

LIMITS ON THE POWER OF
PUBLIC SECURITY INSTITUTIONS

In fulfilling their duties as stipulated by law, public security institutions have the power to take coercive measures. Limits of their power are determined by the nature of their work and the tasks assigned to them. The state vests them with power in the form of law, but also limits their power. Any coercive measures taken by public security institutions must be within the limits of the law.

Public security institutions are one of the most important aspects of the Chinese people's democratic dictatorship. Personnel of public security, including the police, come from the masses. Cultivating flesh-and-blood ties with the masses, public security institutions faithfully protect the lives, property, rights and interests of the people from infringement. Representing the people's interest, public security institutions must not flaunt their authority to create difficulties for the masses. Because their fundamental aim is to serve the people wholeheartedly, public security agencies must understand clearly that the relationship between the people's police and the masses is one between fish and water.

Still, to effectively guard the people's interests, public security institutions must possess special, coercive powers. They are armed administrative institutions maintaining public order in the state. The people's police is a combination of military force with administration.

Public security institutions are special state agencies in charge of public order and state security. The state law assigns to them the duty of organizing the administration of public order.

The public security institutions are also special investigation departments, responsible for investigating criminal cases. To investigate criminal acts, track down criminals, and protect innocent persons from being wronged, they can adopt all types of investigative measures according to legal procedure.

Because of special tasks and the nature of their work, China's public security institutions have the following functions and powers:

The power of criminal investigation They collect and examine evidence, expose crimes, and apprehend criminals according to the Criminal Procedure Law. Public security institutions share the right of investigation with procuratorial institutions in China, although there is division of labor in investigating specific cases. Public security institutions at the county and city level and above are chiefly engaged in investigating counter-revolutionary cases and other major criminal cases such as murder, robbery, rape, arson, etc. Procuratorial institutions are primarily responsible for investigating cases of corruption, malfeasance and infringement of citizens' democratic rights, as well as other cases that are deemed necessary for investigation.

Public security institutions are the primary institutions of criminal investigation. Before conducting an investigation, they carefully examine the evidence. If they discover incriminating evidence, they promptly file a case. If there is no such evidence but a crime has taken place, they should inspect the crime scene. They must file a case for investigation if the scene provides facts conforming to the stipulations of the Criminal Procedure Law.

To solve cases promptly, hunt down criminals, and prevent them from escaping, making false confessions, destroying evidence, or committing further crimes, public security institutions are authorized to inspect, examine and question the defendant or witness, produce expert evidence, search, detain, issue wanted circulars, and hunt down criminals. When necessary, they must take coercive measures to bring offenders into court. They can also release offenders on bail, make house arrest, detain or arrest them.

At the end of an investigation, a public security institution should write opinion for or against prosecution. It is then forwarded along with the related files and evidence to the people's procuratorial institution at the same level for examination and decision.

If the public security institution finds that it is wrong to charge the defendant with criminal responsibility in the course of criminal investigation, it should withdraw the case according to law. If the defendant has already been arrested, release must take place immediately and a certificate of release issued. It should inform the people's court that the public security institution is satisfied that the defendant is innocent.

In the course of a criminal investigation, the public security institution shall not keep the defendant in custody for more than two months. In a complicated case that cannot be solved in two months, the detention period can be extended for one more month with the approval of the superior people's procuratorial office.

In exercising their power of investigation, the public security institutions adopt various measures, such as searching the person, articles, homes and other places in hunting down wanted criminals. These measures often infringe on the right of citizens to inviolable freedom of person and home. Therefore, the investigation must be conducted according to the Criminal Procedure Law.

The power of imposing penalty When a criminal is pronounced guilty and punished according to the Criminal Procedure Law, the public security institution has the right to execute the sentence outside the prison, grant a reprieve, release the offender on parole, put the offender under surveillance and deprive him or her of political rights, detain the offender in custody, or confiscate the offender s property.

Public security institutions should adhere to the principle of revolutionary humanism and carry out a policy of coupling education with reform toward criminals. If a criminal, sentenced to life imprisonment, or some other specified term, or otherwise in custody, is seriously ill and requires treatment outside on bail, or is pregnant, or has to care for her infant child, the public security institution should execute the sentence outside the prison according to stipulations of the Criminal Law.

In executing a sentence outside prison, the public security institution shall entrust surveillance of the criminal to the police station or to a grassroots organization near the home or unit of the criminal. Public security institutions also have the right to supervise criminals released on parole.

The public security institutions also have the right to put known criminals under surveillance and deprive them of political rights. When the term of sentence ends, they shall inform the criminal and the masses of the removal of surveillance, or the restoration of political rights.

When necessary, the public security institutions will execute any sentence of property confiscation jointly with the people's court, regardless of whether it is an independent sentence or an additional sentence.

The power of administering social order Public security institutions enjoy the powers of administering social order, imposing administrative penalties, and holding custodial interrogation.

Administration of social order means the administration of census registration, traffic control, fire prevention, communications and public order. Imposing administrative penalties means meting out administrative punishment to persons who violate rules and regulations for public order without committing any crimes. The public security institutions have the right to inflict various coercive punishment such as re-educating juvenile delinquents through labor, canceling one's residence registration, and imposing other such penalties.

The power of custodial interrogation means temporarily restricting the freedom of a person, and examining those who are suspected of committing major crimes.

Special power in performing duties In case of emergency, the police have the right to use weapons to defend themselves and to physically restrain criminals in the performance of their duties.

In dangerous situations when criminals resist arrest, instigate riots, assault the police, seize fire arms or resort to violence to disturb public order, the police have the right to use arms and weapons to defend themselves and suppress such criminality. The state has strictly provided in legislation that public security institutions and police can use arms and weapons to defend themselves and suppress criminality only by complete conformance to the stipulations of the law.

Necessary power is vested in the public security institutions to perform their duties in the interest of protecting the people. Public security institutions must wield their power lawfully. They are not allowed to transgress the limits prescribed by law or to use their power to create special privileges or take advantage of the people.

People's procuratorial institutions have the right to supervise the investigative activities of public security and punish illegal practices such as extorting confessions by torture and persecuting prisoners. All public security institutions and police must exercise their functions and powers according to the law and adhere to the principle of serving the people.

TASKS OF PUBLIC SECURITY INSTITUTIONS

As an important tool for strengthening the people's democratic dictatorship, the public security institutions play an irreplaceable part in defending the socialist state, protecting its property and the interests of the state, collectives and citizens, ensuring freedom and safety to all, and maintaining normal social production and public order. Nevertheless, the tasks of public security institutions are different at different stages of social development. At present their tasks are to protect the people, crush the enemy, keep public order, and ensure stable conditions for China's modernization.

China's public security institutions have the following specific tasks:

— Guarding against criminal action by counter-revolutionaries;

—Guarding against criminal activities;

—Protecting state property and secrets;

—Performing guard duty;

—Conducting preliminary hearings;

—Controlling urban traffic;

—Engaging in fire prevention work;

—Administering public order and census registration;

— Directing and administering people's armed police and internal security work in frontier defense; and

— Educating, training, assessing and administering cadres and officials and policemen of public security institutions.

The tasks of public security institutions concentrate on preventing, controlling, and handling crimes, acts in violation of public order, and disastrous accidents. The specialized nature of public security institutions cover the following five classifications:

Investigating criminal cases One of the most important specialized tasks of public security institutions is to file cases promptly for investigating various crimes. It includes the following:

Investigating counterrevolutionary cases Public security institutions must fight counterrevolutionaries and promptly investigate and solve counterrevolutionary cases. Such investigation is aimed at effectively exposing, preventing, controlling and suppressing all conspiracies and sabotage.

Investigating ordinary criminal cases According to the stipulations of state laws, public security institutions must adopt specialized investigative means and coercive measures to expose, control, and prevent crime. Such investigation is aimed at effectively stopping, controlling, and punishing serious criminal violence, combating international terrorism, solving criminal cases, stopping the operations of overseas criminal organizations, smuggling groups and underworld societies, and preventing crime in general.

Conducting preliminary hearings for persons arrested and detained according to law Such hearings are a continuation of investigative work and involve examination and interrogation of criminals before they are brought to court for trial. This is an important part of criminal procedure ensuring success in prosecution and trial. During preliminary hearings, public security institutions should gather all the facts surrounding the defendant's behavior, the relationship between the defendant and other criminals in the same case, and ensure that no innocent person shall be charged. In conducting preliminary hearings, the public security institutions must insist on the principle of seeking truth from facts, laying stress on evidence and investigation, and refrain from extorting confessions by force.

Security work This involves economic and cultural security, guard duty, and frontier defense security.

Economic and cultural security These specialized tasks are shared jointly by public security institutions, security departments in economic and cultural areas, and security organizations in factories, mines, businesses, government offices and schools. Cooperating together, these organizations tighten security measures to prevent and control crimes, so that success in production and scientific research can be realized. They also protect state property, state secrets, and vital facilities from disastrous accidents.

Guard duties Public security institutions ensure the safety of the subjects they guard and prevent secret killings, natural accidents, and accidents due to negligence that threaten the safety of the persons and things they guard.

Frontier defense security work This work ensures the territorial integrity and sovereignty of the state, defends the state, and maintains peace and security in border areas.

Census registration A routine function of public security is the compilation of statistics on population growth and the movement of population. Census registration control is an important way to safeguard the legitimate rights and interests of citizens and to prevent, control and discover a variety of criminal activities.

Urban traffic control Maintaining an orderly flow of automotive and pedestrian traffic in cities is one of the key tasks of public security institutions. They should establish a systematic and scientific control of traffic as a means of reducing the death toll on the roads. They should punish persons who violate traffic rules and regulations and those who cause traffic accidents.

The administration of social order Public security institutions have control over some special trades, dangerous goods, and public places to ensure stable public order. They are responsible for safeguarding dangerous objects to prevent both accidents and unlawful use by criminals.

The public security institutions must discharge their duties in accordance with state laws, rules and regulations. Any failure to do so may be reported to the appropriate state authorities by any citizen wishing to file a complaint.

STATE SECURITY INSTITUTIONS

To meet the need of opening to the outside world and strengthening state security against international spies, the First Session of the Sixth NPC approved the establishment of Ministry of State Security. Founded on July 1, 1983, it began to build up a system of state security institutions.

Under the jurisdiction of the State Council, the Ministry of State Security is an institution of the people's democratic dictatorship. To meet the needs of practicality, the ministry has established subordinate institutions in provinces, autonomous regions and municipalities directly under the Central Government, as well as related agencies in places it deems necessary.

The Ministry of State Security is a special security office in charge of investigating spies and secret agents, formerly a task performed by the public security institutions. Hence, the nature of its work is similar to that of the public security institutions. The NPC Standing Committee decided, in September 1983, that state security institutions are authorized to exercise powers granted to the public security institutions by the Constitution and laws, to wit, investigation, detention and arrest of criminals, and the holding of preliminary hearings.

The nature of China's state security institutions determines their key tasks as follows:

Ensuring the safety of the state Established for this purpose in the light of the open door policy and other new international developments, the state security institutions must take practical and effective measures to ensure the stability and security of the state by preventing foreign inspired conspiracies, subversion, and sabotage.

Strengthening anti-espionage work Espionage and counterespionage activities have intensified as the global situation becomes increasingly complex. As China opens to the outside world in pursuit of the open door policy, some foreign espionage agencies have intensified their efforts to obtain military and economic intelligence here. Their activities include attempting to procure state secrets and infiltrating China with spies to subvert the People's Republic. State security institutions must adopt effective measures and use proper technical equipment to combat these covert activities. They must exercise the people's democratic dictatorship to crack down the conspiratorial activities of international spies and secret agents, and to undermine counterrevolutionary acts aimed at jeopardizing state security.

CHAPTER 10

Administration of Justice

The administration of justice in China is carried out by the Ministry of Justice. The system of judicial administration was established in the early years of the 1950s when the Central People's Government established the Ministry of Justice. Subsequently, departments for the administration of justice were established in the provinces, autonomous regions, municipalities directly under the Central Government, and in the prefectural commissioners' offices. Then the Ministry of Justice of the Central People's Government changed its name to the Ministry of Justice of the People's Republic of China in accordance with the 1954 Constitution. Bureaus for the administration of justice were established in each province, autonomous region, and municipality directly under the Central Government. And in prefectural commissioners' offices and in the people's courts at the grassroots level, sub-divisional offices were founded to handle the work of judicial administration. In this way, a set of laws governing the administration of justice began to be developed.

In 1959, the Ministry of Justice and its departments at different levels were eliminated. Their work was taken over by the Supreme People's Court and the people's courts of the higher levels for administration and management.

To strengthen the building of socialism, democracy, and a socialist legal system, the Eleventh Session of the Fifth NPC Standing Committee decided on September 13, 1979 to re-establish the Ministry of Justice. As a result, departments for judicial administration at different levels were established in all areas. Thus, a system for judicial administration was gradually restored from the lowest level to the Central Government.

In China, the Ministry of Justice is under the direct leadership of the State Council. This arrangement allows representatives of the State Council to guide and supervise the professional work and policies of the judicial administrative departments at different levels.

Judicial administrative departments at different levels are under the leadership of the people's governments at their corresponding levels. At the same time, however, they accept supervision and guidance in their professional work and policy decisions from the departments above and from the Ministry of Justice.

At present, the responsibilities and organizational structure of the judicial administrative departments are in the process of revision. Major areas of reform are in training officials, disseminating legal knowledge and improving legal education. The Ministry of Justice also focuses on reform in the provision of legal services, notary services and arbitration, in the work of the prisons and reform through labor institutions, in judicial administration of foreign matters, and in the research and development of policies in judicial administration.

CHARACTERISTICS

Since 1979, significant developments have been made in judicial administration in China. The 1982 Constitution clearly stipulates that the State Council is in charge of managing the judicial administration, from establishing judicial administrative work to giving this work legal recognition. The primary task of judicial administration in China is to serve the country. In so doing, the work of judicial administration also fosters economic development and the development of democracy. This leads to long-term stability for China and serves the Chinese people better.

For economic development On October 20, 1984, the Third Plenary Session of the Twelfth CPC Congress convened to discuss regulations pertaining to the economic reforms. Flourishing economic activities led the congress to decide that a set of legal criteria is necessary both to facilitate reforms and development of China's economy.

The Ministry of Justice carries out this policy by vigorously providing the legal services needed for the reconstruction of the economy. In recent years, judicial administrative departments in China have actively accomplished the following tasks:

—Qualified personnel have been vigorously trained in the field of economic law.

—Labor reform enterprises and reform through labor institutions have persevered in upgrading education first and increasing economic benefits second.

—Economic rules and regulations like economic contract law have been disseminated.

—In the work of the people's mediation, priority has been given to economic issues so that production is not hindered.

—The focal point of notary work is in the area of economic contracts.

—Lawyers provide legal consultation and services to economic work units, rural households engaged in specialized production and those working in the united economic compounds.

—In the work of judicial administration of foreign matters, every available channel is used to disseminate knowledge on the significant achievements made within the Chinese legal system, which makes it easy for the introduction of foreign capital, technology and advanced equipment.

For the establishment of a legal system in a socialist democracy The fundamental direction of judicial administrative work is the work of building socialism on one hand and developing law on the other hand. Its chief task is to serve the development of socialist democracy on the one hand and the perfection of socialist legal system on the other. To accomplish this important task, the judicial administrative departments have worked conscientiously in the following areas:

—Major efforts have been made in the development of legal education and in the development and training of cadres and officials. This work is an essential step in the development of socialist democracy and strengthens the construction of the legal

138

system. A comprehensive program for legal education plus well-trained cadres and officials is necessary for the rational and proportionate development of administrative departments in the cities. With well-trained cadres and officials, the creation of administrative departments can be expedited and their developments made more harmonious.

—Rules and regulations for judicial administration are being strengthened and developed. In the judicial administrative departments, efforts are made for greater efficiency. Legal knowledge is to be disseminated by these departments to the people, as knowledge of the law leads to better compliance of the law.

—Major developments have taken place in legal and notary services. Following the spirit of reform, progress has been made both in the development of professional lawyers and part-time lawyers and in building a network among them. Similarly, notaries and notary liaison personnel are developing their own network. This type of networking is another step in improving China's system of lawyers and notaries.

—For more realistic legislative reforms, proposals, and judicial administrative policies, more energy is directed to research and development of theoretical work in judicial administration.

For the long-term stability of the country Socialist modernization cannot be achieved without stability and unity among all aspects of society. Development of a prosperous and thriving economy in China cannot be guaranteed if there is no stability. For the achievement of long-term stability, the judicial administrative departments should concentrate their efforts in the following areas:

—In reform through labor, labor reform sites should rehabilitate as well as punish offenders so that they can become law-abiding citizens. Those who undergo reform through labor are generally minor criminals and juvenile delinquents. Labor reform institutions should treat juvenile delinquents in their custody the way parents treat a sick child, or the way a doctor treats his patient, or the way a teacher treats an erring student. Only by adopting this outlook can conditions be created to accelerate the process of reforming delinquents.

—A general knowledge of law should be made popular among the people. In broadening the public's knowledge of law, attention must be given to the method in which law is disseminated to ensure that it is accurate, lively and sound. The dissemination of law to the masses should be systematized and regularized into a daily exercise so that everyone's concept of law, from the masses to the cadres and officials, will be broadened.

—Progress in mediation is under way. The people's mediation should use preventive measures in their work. When preventive measures are given priority and disputes mediated by law, right can be distinguished from wrong and the rights and interests of the people are preserved.

For the service of the people   The judicial administrative departments and their personnel are public servants. Their work is in the service of the masses and follows the dictatorship of the masses. Therefore, the work of the judicial administrative departments and their personnel has the following features:

—After office hours, the personnel of judicial administrative departments are encouraged to disseminate legal knowledge in the city streets and provide legal consultation in the villages at the county level.

—Notaries and judicial administrative personnel are organized for tours of villages and counties to provide more extensive legal services to the people.

—Judicial administrative departments establish legal service stations in villages and counties. These stations disseminate legal knowledge, provide legal consultation and notary services. They also assist in the further development of the people's mediation.

—Lawyers are invited to act as legal consultants to rural households engaged in specialized production.

LEGAL EDUCATION AND THE TRAINING OF CADRES AND OFFICIALS

Since the founding of the People's Republic, legal education and the training of cadres and officials have had many ups and downs. The China University of Political Science and Law was founded in 1949. A year later it opened the China Research Institute for New Legal Studies and the Central Judicial Administration Training Classes for Cadres and Officials. After the

People's University and the Northeast People's University were established, they respectively set up law departments and enrolled undergraduate students. In 1951, the Central Cadres and Officials School of Political Science and Law was also founded to train personnel for the work of judicial administration.

At the same time, reforms were implemented in colleges and universities across the country. The old legal educational programs in the colleges and universities were revised. Of all the law departments at universities and law institutes, only eight were maintained and the remainder were either eliminated or merged with other organizations. Of the eight that remained, they are law departments at the People's University, the Northeast People's University, Wuhan University, the Northwest China Institute of Political Science and Law, Beijing Institute of Political Science and Law, the East China College of Political Science and Law, the South China College of Political Science and Law, and the Southwest China Institute of Political Science and Law. Each of these departments and institutes revised their curriculum, discarding many unnecessary and cumbersome course materials. Unfortunately the overall arrangement lacked a comprehensive and rational design which proved to be a detriment to legal education.

In 1954, a national meeting on education in political science and law was held. At this meeting, educators met to exchange experiences in legal education and to formulate policies in legal education and define its tasks. They decided that legal education could best be furthered by establishing additional law departments at universities and law institutes with development in their curriculum. This resulted in the establishment of law departments at Beijing University, Fudan University and the Northwest University. By 1957, ten more law departments and law institutes were founded, including four institutes of political science and law and six law departments in colleges and universities. In the institutes and law departments, there were a total of 6,152 teachers and students, which amounted to 1.4 percent of the national total of teachers and students in institutes of higher learning. After 1957, legal education sustained a series of setbacks. During the "cultural revolution," legal education ground to a halt.

Since the Third Plenary Session in 1978, legal education, judicial administration, and training of cadres and officials have all been restored and further developed. As it appears now, even greater progress will be made in each of these areas.

Legal education in colleges and universities has been restored and developed By the end of 1978, four institutes of political science and law, the Beijing Institute, the East China College, the Northwest China Institute and the Southwest China Institute, and the law department of the People's University, began enrolling students. From 1979 onwards, law departments at Beijing University and Wuhan University offered courses in law as a major field of study and thirty other universities followed suit, establishing law departments. In 1983, Beijing Institute of Political Science and Law obtained approval to establish the China University of Political Science and Law. By the end of 1984, China had thirty-seven law departments, institutes and schools in its colleges and universities, which is three times greater than the number in 1957. The distribution of law departments and their branch offices and institutes has become gradually more equitable. In terms of research fellows with masters and doctorate degrees engaged in further research in various legal topics, the number has doubled since 1957. Furthermore, groups of teachers and students of law have been sent abroad for further studies.

Additionally, in the past few years, some places have established a group of legal training schools. In several financial and economic institutes, institutes for nationalities and teachers training colleges, majors in law, economic law and international law were established to faster the training of personnel conversant in both law and economics.

Legal education in secondary schools is being improved Legal education in China's secondary schools has always been weak. The internal structure of legal education is not well organized resulting in an imbalance in the proportion of institutes of higher learning to secondary schools. In recent years, there has been some improvement and several judicial administration schools have been established. By the end of 1984, twenty-eight schools of judicial administration have been established in China's twenty-four provinces, autonomous regions and municipalities directly under the Central Government. These schools have trained more than two thousand middle level personnel and have a current student population of six thousand. Many additional channels for legal education and training are available, such as training classes at the schools of judicial administration, vocational law schools, and high schools of law. Correspondence courses and television courses in secondary level legal training are offered in some areas.

Developments in legal education Many types of developments are taking place in legal education as China gradually broadens legal education in the institutes of higher learning as well as in the schools at the secondary and vocational training levels. To train legal personnel quickly and economically, many different educational methods have been adopted. In the last few years, branch universities and short-term professional colleges have developed very rapidly and although no accurate statistics have been taken, there are, by approximation, some twenty-odd short-term professional colleges, law departments and training classes already in operation at various branch universities. This kind of school is increasingly becoming an important channel for replenishing legal preparatory personnel.

China has also begun to raise the level of spare-time and after-work-hours legal education in all locales. At present, the China Institute of Political Science and Law, the Southwest China Institute of Political Science and Law and the South China College of Political Science and Law offer legal training through correspondence courses. With a combined student population of over ten thousand, these institutes already have two thousand graduates from their correspondence courses. In addition, the People's University, Jilin University, Zhengzhou University, Anhui University and Xiangtan University all offer legal training through correspondence courses. There are also television universities, night universities, do-it-yourself examination course and others of this type of legal education.

Gradual standardization of the training of cadres and officials In recent years, the Ministry of Justice has attached great importance to the professional training of cadres and officials. To achieve this aim, it has gradually established a three-tier training system in the Central Government, the provinces and

143

localities. Beginning with short-term training programs, the focus gradually shifted to a standardized training program. At present, apart from the Central Judicial Administration Training School for Cadres and Officials and the Central Cadres and Officials Institute of Management of Reform Through Labor at the first tier, each province, autonomous region and municipality under the Central Government has established approximately thirty institutes of management of political science and law and twenty-three schools to train cadres and officials for work in reform through labor institutions. In localities, cities and prefectures, seventy-six institutes of political science and law or training classes for cadres and officials have been established. By the end of 1984, two hundred thousand judicial administration personnel have been trained in short-term training courses in schools for cadres and officials at each tier.

In December 1983, the Ministry of Justice and the Ministry of Education (now called the State Education Commission) opened a nationwide symposium on legal education. At the symposium, the developmental environment for legal education in China, the importance of research in legal educational policies and tentative plans for further development were discussed. Views expressed brought out the need to modernize legal education in China so as to be consistent with modern realities while building socialist modernization and a corresponding legal system. Other views expressed included the need to increase China's financial resources, the need to increase both the quantity and quality of qualified teachers and to give first priority to the development of institutes of political science and law and schools for the training of cadres and officials so that more administrative levels and regulations, and more methods of legal education and cadre and official training can be developed. With the accomplishment of these objectives in mind, before the end of 1990, basic facilities should be available to satisfy the needs of legal education and the training of cadres and officials so that after 1990, there will be legal expertise able to prepare for the conditions that will arise as China enters a new phase of rapid economic development. Most recently, besides diligently establishing schools and institutes of law and increasing student enrollment, the major areas for growth are: increasing the number of graduate students and undergraduate courses; developing secondary education, television universities, correspondence universities, night universities, do-it-yourself examination courses and other types of legal education; and exerting major efforts into training professional cadres and officials to staff and develop administrative positions in a harmonious and rational manner.

DISSEMINATION OF LEGAL KNOWLEDGE

Legal knowledge is disseminated through the legislature, the tribunals, the procuratorates, government institutions and social organizations. The judicial administrative organizations and their leaders should make greater efforts in the dissemination of legal knowledge. In the 1950s, the judicial administrative departments successfully popularized the Constitution among the people. But from 1957 onward and especially during the "cultural revolution," along with the weakening of the socialist legal system, hardly any legal knowledge was disseminated among the people. Since the 1978 Third Plenary Session, there have been profound and extensive developments in the legal system and in basic legal instruction for the public. In the past few years, legal instruction has grown from teaching law to individuals to an integrated system of public legal education so that all citizens will have a better concept of their legal system.

To carry out the dissemination of legal knowledge in every area of law and the legal system China has recently issued the Constitution as well as a series of other important laws. To accomplish the important task of disseminating legal knowledge, the judicial administrative offices work arduously and adopt various means of instruction. Often, unusual methods such as organized activities of all kinds are used as a means of legal instruction. On December 10, 1982, the Ministry of Justice asked its departments at different levels to organize immediately a short-term personnel training program. Graduates of this program would go to factories, mines, commercial enterprises, villages, small towns and schools to teach basic laws and the legal system to the public. In their teaching, the instructors from the judicial administrative departments should focus on reality and practice so that the students can have a greater awareness of the legal system and the concept of democracy.

From the second half of 1979 to 1982, China's judicial administrative departments appropriately focused their attention on criminal law and criminal procedure law. In handling criminal matters, they asked each locale to use typical cases for guidance and to take into consideration the immediate existing problems. In terms of public legal instruction, each locale should use methods and organize activities that can be easily comprehensible to the public. To realize the work of public legal instruction, it was necessary for some cities and regions to integrate and reorganize for social stability. Likewise, it was necessary for factories to link up and reorganize for labor discipline, villages to join together for their social customs and schools to work together for the implementation of student regulations. At the same time, marriage law, civil procedure law, economic contract law, military service law and the laws governing national autonomous regions should also be reorganized.

To disseminate a general knowledge of law to the public For thousands of years China was a feudal state. Lacking a democratic tradition and without a developed concept of a legal system, many Chinese citizens lack familiarity with the law and have not developed a sense of reliance on the law. In June 1984, the justice department in Benxi, a medium-sized city in Liaoning Province, called for a symposium on the systematic dissemination of general knowledge in the law and the legal syste. The intention of this symposium is to develop a more systematic approach to public legal instruction in China. At the symposium, it was proposed that after a year of preparations and within five years, all Chinese citizens should have a basic general knowledge of law.

In June 1985, a nationwide symposium opened in Beijing on the dissemination of legal knowledge and education. This symposium formulated a program for instructing the public in basic legal topics. This program involves systematic basic instruction in the areas of the Constitution, criminal law and criminal procedure law, civil procedure law, marriage law, inheritance law, economic contract law, military service law, sentencing regula-

146

tions, public order and stability laws and laws in other areas related to the lives of the people. This program, which runs from 1985 to 1990, requires the determination of the most important target areas for disseminating legal knowledge. To make this determination, the program suggests the need to consider the differences between regions, in the work of the cadres and officials and in the needs of the people. Of course, other basic measures and methods must be taken into account.

To establish classes in law at all types of schools and at all levels Since 1982, several elementary schools in the cities and provinces of Liaoning, Jilin, Yunnan, etc. have started experimental units and have organized a set of teaching materials for their respective regions. In July 1985, the State Education Commission, together with the Ministry of Justice, called a symposium on legal education in elementary schools nationwide to discuss the curriculum for legal education in elementary schools. It was decided that moral ideological instruction is the basis for legal education in elementary schools. Along with teaching the rudiments of law, teachers must cultivate in their students a sense of ideals and ethical behavior as well as literacy and discipline which are needed for the long-term stability of the country.

Except for a few in remote regions, all Chinese middle schools, from 1982 onward, offer classes in general law. In Jinan, Shandong Province, in October 1984, a nationwide symposium on legal education in middle schools was held. Conferees at this symposium exchanged teaching experiences and discussed improving teaching methods and areas for further development.

In recent years, colleges and universities, especially liberal arts and teachers' colleges and universities, have gradually begun to offer classes in law and the legal system so that 249 colleges and universities now offer such courses. This year, the State Education Commission, together with the Ministry of Justice, decided to ask all colleges and universities to begin gradually offering courses in law and the legal system.

To establish legal newspapers and periodicals At the end of 1979, the Ministry of Justice decided to establish *China Legal System*, the first legal newspaper of its kind, which began domestic publication on August 1, 1980, followed by a Hong

147

Kong, Macao and overseas edition beginning on January 1, 1981. With a circulation of over ten thousand copies, the *China Legal System* has an extensive readership. At the same time, from 1980 onward, each province, autonomous region and municipality directly under the Central Government has also begun gradually publishing legal newspapers and twelve cities with a population exceeding one million have founded legal newspapers.

The Legal Press of the Ministry of Justice founded both *Legal System Building* and *Law and Life*. *Legal System Building* is a specialized publication for legal professionals while *Law and Life* aims to broaden the legal knowledge of cadres, officials and the general public with a special emphasis on instructing younger people on general aspects of law. Published under the direction of the judicial administration departments, these two monthly periodicals had over nine hundred thousand copies printed in each period in 1985.

Along with reconstruction and development of the legal system, several legal research institutions and organizations have been set up.

To increase legal publications In the period following the founding of the People's Republic, there were no publishing organizations for professional literature. Legal publications were handled through an editor's office at the People's Press. In 1954, the Legal Press was established and in 1956 it came under the jurisdiction of the Ministry of Justice. From 1954 to 1960, it published over four hundred kinds of books, the most important of which were translations of works by foreign jurists, *Laws and Regulations of the People's Republic of China* and other regulations and legal materials. Afterwards, the Legal Press became defunct but was restored in June 1980. In recent years, the Legal Press edited laws and regulations, and published all types of materials for legal studies and scholarship, including a number of academic works and translations as well as legal materials for general readership. However, even in this prolific period of publications, legal books are still very difficult to obtain, especially for those in the rural areas. This problem of access needs urgent resolution.

FOREIGN EXCHANGE WORK IN
THE JUDICIAL ADMINISTRATIVE DEPARTMENTS

China's judicial administrative departments have been very active in the area of foreign exchanges in the past few years and have worked for closer ties and more exchanges with their counterparts in foreign countries. To improve mutual understanding they work to promote exchanges of books and materials with personnel and delegations from international judicial administrative organizations. This work aids the construction of a socialist legal system and economy and promotes world peace and progress.

Major areas of foreign exchange work of China's judicial administrative departments are:

—Participation in international activities related to judicial administration;

—Participation in the United Nations international conferences on human rights and crime prevention;

—Sending personnel or delegations to international judicial administrative organizations;

—Negotiating and discussing questions and problems in judicial administration with other countries or their representative organizations;

— Negotiating and concluding agreements with foreign countries in the area of judicial administration;

—Sending Chinese judicial administration personnel, delegations, organizations and study groups abroad;

— Inviting and receiving domestic and foreign judicial administration personnel, delegations and organizations;

—Sending experts and academics abroad to lecture and for further study;

— Working with related departments in informing foreign countries of the construction of a socialist legal system;

—Working with foreign countries to exchange and develop legal books, materials and information in judicial administration; and

—Conducting research and study on the legal system and judicial administration in every country.

Relations and exchanges with international judicial admini-stration organizations In the last few years, China has spon-sored and attended United Nations international conferences. For example, in 1980, the Chinese judicial administration dele-gation attended the United Nations Sixth Conference on Crime Prevention and Treatment of Criminals held in Caracas, Venezuela. In May 1984, for the first time, Beijing sponsored the preparatory meeting for the United Nations Seventh Regional Conference for Crime Prevention and Treatment of Criminals. In September 1985, the Chinese judicial administration delega-tion attended the United Nations Seventh Conference on Crime Prevention and Treatment of Criminals held in Milan, Italy, and in 1982, the Ministry of Justice sent representatives to the 38th Conference of the United Nations Commission on Human Rights. In 1983, the Chinese delegation participated in the seven international conferences among which were: three conferences on human rights and crime prevention called by the United Na-tions, and four other international conferences on matters con-cerning judicial administration. In 1984 the Chinese delegation attended the 40th Conference of the United Nations Commis-sion on Human Rights, the United Nations Eighth Conference on Crime Prevention and Control, the Fifth Pre-conference Preparatory Meeting of the United Nations Seventh Conference for Crime Prevention and Treatment of Criminals, and other in-ternational conferences on matters of judicial administration.

At the same time, China also participated in and became involved with the activities of other international judicial admin-istration organizations. For example, for the first time in 1982, the Chinese delegation registered to run for election at the United Nations Commission on Crime Prevention and Control, and at the Spring Meeting of the United Nations Economic and Social Council, the Chinese delegation was elected. In 1982, Chinese representatives held the post of reporter at the United Nations Crime Prevention Conference. In 1983, the Chinese del-egation attended the Conference of the International Associa-tion on Constitutional Law and, for the first time, used an inter-national constitutional law forum to introduce Chinese constitu-tional law on the one hand, while obtaining a better under-standing of international constitutional law and its trends and developments on the other. Reference materials and academic works were exchanged at the conference. In 1983, China also participated in the International Conference on Information Data and Material for Judicial Administration to understand better the most up-to-date information, the latest developments and the newest scientific materials and data for judicial administration. In 1984, China attended the International Conference on Criminal Law.

To have exchanges and relations with every country After the founding of the PRC, the judicial administrative departments once organized a delegation of judicial administration personnel in the 1950s to go abroad to promote exchanges, understanding and friendship among countries. In the past few years, China has promoted even more exchanges and contacts with countries all over the world. For example, in 1981, China sent a delegation to Thailand and Sri Lanka; in 1982, China sent a judicial administration delegation to Romania, Yugoslavia and Japan. In 1983, the Chinese judicial administration delegation went to Belgium, Italy and Japan to invite the Minister of Justice of each of these countries to visit China and also called on India, Australia, New Zealand, West Germany, etc. In 1984, the Chinese delegations called on Thailand, Australia, Algeria and Omen, and in 1985 and thereafter, more and more delegations have been sent abroad. During these visits, the Chinese delegations observed and studied the judicial administration systems of the host countries for a better understanding of their judicial administration systems, the work of their lawyers and their legal education systems. By learning about the experiences of different countries in judicial administration and drawing from their materials and data, China can build its own socialist legal system more effectively.

During this period, the Chinese judicial administrative departments have cordially invited and received visiting foreign judicial administration delegations, organizations and personnel. In 1980, Chinese judicial administrative departments invited and received five judicial administration delegations from abroad: a delegation of justices from Malta's highest court; a research and study delegation from Thailand; the Minister of Justice from Rwanda; the ministers of justice from Trinidad and Tobago; and

151

a delegation from Sri Lanka. In 1981, China hosted eleven judicial administration delegations from Singapore, Thailand, the United States, Japan, France, Great Britain, Switzerland, Canada and Australia, and in 1982 received twenty-three delegations worldwide including those from Thailand, Yugoslavia, Romania, Ecuador, Australia, Sri Lanka, Omen, Japan, the Philippines, India, Belgium, Switzerland, Sweden and the United States. In 1983, China received judicial administration delegations from many regions, including those from India, Thailand, Zimbabwe, Japan, New Zealand, Romania, North Korea, Sri Lanka, Belgium and the United States as well as regional judicial administration consultation delegations from the United Nations Crime Prevention and Criminal Affairs Organization, etc. In 1984, China hosted some thirty delegations including those from Belgium, Hong Kong, Japan, Romania, the United States, Yugoslavia, Australia, New Zealand, Austria, Sweden, Hungary, India and West Germany. In some of these delegations were the vice-premier of Belgium who is also the head of the department for judicial administration and reform, the Swedish Minister of Justice, the Minister of Justice of Yugoslavia, the Australian Minister of Justice, the West German Secretary of Justice, the Dean of the Institute of Legislative Law of France, the former deputy justice of Japan's highest court, the present legal counsel to the crown prince of Japan and the head of the American Lawyers Association. In the last few years, as a result of closer ties between China and the countries of the world, exchanges have become even more extensive. Guests and friends from abroad who have visited China for a deeper understanding of its legal system have shown appreciation for the gains and accomplishments made. They have also given high acclaim to the work of the people's mediation and to the work of reforming and rehabitating criminals.

To strengthen foreign exchanges in legal education and research and to promote academic exchanges with every country Recently, China have begun sending experts and scholars overseas to teach and to engage in research in areas of law that are relevant to China. These Chinese experts and scholars disseminate knowledge about the Chinese legal system during their stay abroad. This type of exchange is rare since 1949. For example, the year 1983 marked the first time the Ministry of Justice and the law schools sent students abroad for advanced studies. Some went to American law schools, some left for special universities in Belgium, while others attended the United Nations Crime Prevention Research Program for Far East Asia. Still others were awarded the United Nations Human Rights Scholarship for further studies in France. Chinese legal scholars also went to Columbia University's Law School and to Japan Comparative Law Research Institute for further studies. In 1984, more than ten renowned professors and research fellows were sent by the judicial administrative departments to thirteen different organizations in the United States, Belgium and West Germany for further studies and research.

Foreign exchanges in legal education and research have two objectives. One is to introduce China's legal system and economic construction as well as the accomplishments they have made. The other is to study the theoretical and practical aspects of foreign legal systems that may be relevant to China, to promote academic exchanges and mutual understanding in scholarship that is universally beneficial.

Meanwhile, China has also received legal experts who have come here. In 1984, four famous Belgian professors gave lectures at the China University of Political Science and Law and the East China College of Political Science and Law while an American professor also lectured at the former. Although this type of exchange has just commenced, it is hoped that in the future, more foreign experts, scholars and organizations will be invited to China by the educational and academic research departments to lecture or to engage in further research and studies.

CHAPTER 11

Reform Through Labor

Reform through labor is the process of reform by which criminals are remolded into useful people for society through collective, productive labor, coupled with political and ideological education, and the learning of general knowledge and production skills. This method of reform involves the following four aspects:

— In punishing criminals, the aim is to reform through compulsory labor, so as to provide them with an opportunity for a new lease on life. Under the exercise of people's democratic political power, this process provides the criminals with the knowledge that hopeful future within the socialist system can be realized as long as they mend their ways.

— In subjecting criminals to labor reform, the reform through labor institutions should be humanitarian. They should protect and respect the rights of the person and the democratic rights of those criminals sentenced to an indefinite term of imprisonment. Criminals should be treated humanely in their food allowance, accommodation, clothing, medical service, and sanitation. Time for rest and work safety must also be provided.

—Effective measures should be taken to educate the criminals. Proceeding from the political aim of educating and remolding the criminals into new people, labor reform institutions should conduct effective political and ideological education to teach general knowledge and production skills.

—Productive labor is the basic means of reforming criminals. Only by participation in socialist collective labor can criminals understand the shamefulness of living a parasitic life. They should be encouraged to foster love for labor by learning the skills of production, so that they can share the common feelings of the laboring people.

China's reform of criminals through labor is different from "penal servitude" and "compensation through labor" of some Western countries. Aimed to remold criminals into new people, it is a judicial process with uniquely Chinese characteristics. China has achieved remarkable progress in the reform of criminals since 1949. After undergoing reform through labor, large numbers of criminals have become technical workers, engineers, doctors, and laborers with certain types of production skills. In this regard, China's effort has won high praise both at home and abroad.

ESTABLISHMENT AND DEVELOPMENT OF THE REFORM THROUGH LABOR SYSTEM

Back in the 1930s during the period of the Second Revolutionary Civil War, there was a labor reform division under the people's justice committee of the provisional central government in the Chinese Soviet. During the Anti-Japanese War, there were labor reform institutes and criminal rehabilitation institutions under the judicial institutions in revolutionary base areas; and in the People's War of Liberation, there were criminal self-education and rehabilitation institutes.

Even then, labor was regarded as the fundamental tool for reforming criminals. Reform through labor comes from the belief that education in basic literacy skills and re-education in the "work is honorable" ethic will successfully reform criminals.

After the founding of the People's Republic, reform through labor institutions were placed under the Ministry of Justice. The main task then was to thoroughly transform the old prisons taken over from the Kuomintang and build a new prison system. Reform Through Labor Regulations of the People's Republic of China were promulgated in September 1954. The regulations have served as the basic guidelines for China's work of labor reform. They have specific provisions as to the nature of

155

labor reform work, its tasks, principles, and policies. The regulations issued for the first time the guiding principle for the work of reform through labor.

Article 4 of the regulations provides that "In carrying out the reform of counterrevolutionaries and all other criminals through labor, reform through labor institutions should follow the principle of combining punishment with ideological transformation and production labor with political education." The promulgation of the regulations signaled a new stage for China's work of reform through labor.

Work in this respect, however, suffered interference from erroneous ideologies and was disrupted from 1966 to 1976. Since the late 1978, however, the Chinese Government has done a great deal in restoring, consolidating, and improving the reform through labor institutions and the relevant system of supervision in eliminating the remaining influence of the Lin Biao and Jiang Qing counterrevolutionary cliques in the work of labor reform, and in strengthening the system of reform through ideological remolding and productive labor.

The Eighth National Conference on the Work of Labor Reform held in 1981 summed up the experiences and lessons in the work of reform through labor since the 1950s, readjusted reform policies in the light of the new conditions in the treatment of criminals, and determined the tasks for reform through labor in the new historical period.

In April 1983, the reform through labor institutions were placed under the Ministry of Justice, bringing about new circumstances in the work of labor reform. The institutions in charge of labor reform were determined to transform themselves gradually into special schools for remolding criminals.

Over the past few years, jurists from many countries have visited China's prisons, factories, and farms involved in labor reform. They were greatly surprised by the constructive work done by China in reforming criminals through labor. They said that China's practice of reforming criminals through labor embodied an effective guideline for "re-education" and praised China's penal system as "admirable." They also said, "Chinese criminals should be proud of themselves as Chinese, because in this society they can have more opportunities than any other place in the world to thoroughly change themselves. Labor reform is a great contribution China is making to the civilization of mankind." A Canadian jurist made the following comments after visiting Chinese prisons: "According to Marxism, criminals can be reformed. The low rate of criminals committing a new crime in your country has proved this." He continued: "You are quite experienced, and very scientific in your management. Your work is very successful. Conceivably your results are better than ours, because yours is a socialist country."

TASKS AND ORGANIZATION OF REFORM THROUGH LABOR INSTITUTIONS

Prisons are places for imprisoning criminals. This has been true both in ancient times and today, and both at home and abroad. In this sense, China's reform through labor institutions are the same as prisons and labor reform teams. But they are not just state criminal institutions and places for punishing offenders; they are also political melting pots for remolding the ideologies of criminals and special schools where criminals may learn general knowledge as well as scientific and technological knowledge. This is an important feature distinguishing Chinese labor reform institutions from the prisons of other countries. Article 2 of the Reform Through Labor Regulations provides that "Reform through labor institutions of the People's Republic of China are one of the tools of the people's democratic dictatorship for punishing and reforming all counterrevolutionaries and other criminals." This provision designates the nature of labor reform institutions in China and specifies their fundamental task. Specifically, China's reform through labor institutions have the following characteristics:

Wide representation Labor reform institutions or teams, in applying criminal punishment to offenders, represent the will and interests of the people, the majority of the population. Their punishment of criminals serves only as a prerequisite and necessary means for reforming them through labor. Their aim is to enable criminals to become new people. This is determined by the historical mission of the working class to transform society

157

and mankind, and is a major characteristic of the China's labor reform institutions.

From 1950 to March 1954, China imprisoned 1,109 Japanese war criminals. They had perpetrated heinous crimes against the Chinese people by applying their policy of "killing all, burning all, and looting all" during the Japanese invasion of China. Incomplete statistics showed that 973 of these war criminals killed a total of 949,814 Chinese, burned down 19,503 houses and looted 36,914,899 tons of grain. According to provisions of both international and Chinese laws, it was necessary to put these war criminals on trial and subject them to criminal punishment. Most even deserved the death penalty in the light of the horror they perpetrated. The Chinese Government did not take nationalistic reprisals against them, but tried to reform them through labor. Success was achieved in the reform of these Japanese war criminals through a fairly long period of meticulous re-education and reform, winning favorable international comments. The majority of the one thousand or so war criminals were pardoned, and repatriated to Japan in 1956. After returning home, most of them took an active part in Japan-China friendship activities. They established the Liaison Committee of the Repatriates from China in Tokyo with fifty-four branches in Japan and they collectively joined the Japan-China Friendship Association. These ex-criminals are now advanced in age, but they still remember the re-education given them by the Chinese people. In August 1980, they sent a delegation made up of their children to visit China, demanding that their children carry on in the cause of friendship between Japanese and Chinese peoples.

China's labor reform institutions do not simply imprison offenders and execute the legally-prescribed sentence; they also try to educate them to abandon evil, do good, and turn over a new leaf.

The fundamental task The fundamental task of China's labor reform institutions is to apply criminal punishment to offenders and reform them. Specifically, they should exercise strict control over criminals serving a sentence and closely integrate criminal punishment with ideological remolding and productive labor with political education. The objective is to enable criminals to undergo reform consciously. They should do their best to

158

turn passive factors into positive ones and remold criminals into new people who support the socialist system, have certain labor skills, and are useful for the country's modernization drive. China's prisons and labor reform institutions are special institutions for executing punitive control of criminals according to law.

To apply punitive control, labor reform institutions jail offenders according to sentences pronounced by the people's courts. Through armed surveillance and political management, they exercise strict control over criminals and restrict their freedom, so as to isolate them from conditions existing in the society for committing a crime. Strict punitive control also allows offenders to understand the severity of the law, reflect on the crimes they have committed so as to admit their crimes, obey the law, and undergo reform to begin a new life. This is one of the tasks of the Chinese institutions of reform through labor.

Another important task of the Chinese labor reform institutions is to organize criminals to engage in large scale socialized production, undergo political and ideological, as well as cultural and technical education, so as to truly renounce evil both in ideology and action. While implementing the law, China's labor reform institutions should employ scientific approaches in reform through labor and education. Consequently, philosophy, education, ethics, sociology, psychology and other scientific knowledge provide guidelines for the reform of criminals through labor.

The organizational structure The organizational structure of China's reform through labor institutions takes different forms. After overthrowing the old political power, China established different types of labor reform institutions to facilitate investigation, adjudication and reform, according to the nature of the crimes and terms of sentences. Chapter 2 of the Reform Through Labor Regulations provides that China's reform through labor institutions consist of detention houses, prisons, labor reform teams and juvenile correctional institutions.

Detention houses Detention houses are mainly used to detain criminals before they are convicted. Part of the labor reform institutions, they are places for detaining criminals, same as prisons, reform through labor teams, and correctional institutions for juvenile offenders. Detention houses are built at the provincial, city, prefectural and county levels. Their working personnel consist of the head, one or two deputy heads, and a number of clerks and custodians. According to Article 8 of the Reform Through Labor Regulations, criminals sentenced to less than two years of imprisonment not eligible for placement in labor reform teams may be transferred to the detention houses, so those imprisoned in detention houses also include some convicted criminals.

Prisons Prisons are used mainly to supervise and control those criminals who are unfit to serve their sentences outside prison. Prisons are established in accordance with the actual needs of the provinces, autonomous regions and municipalities directly under the Central Government, and they are under the jurisdiction of the judicial administrative departments of the provinces, autonomous regions and municipalities directly under the Central Government. Their personnel consist of a head, one or two deputy heads, and staff members in the administrative, education, production, financial affairs, and supply and marketing departments.

Labor reform teams According to Article 17 of the Reform Through Labor Regulations, labor reform teams are to supervise and control criminals who are fit to serve their sentences outside prison. Labor reform teams may be established as general, sub-general, and major teams which are all independent. Small and average teams may be set up under the general, sub-general and major teams based on the number of criminals and needs of production. Average teams are basic grassroots units. The basic work of the labor reform teams is done by "average teams." Under the general, sub-general and major teams, there are administrative, education, production, financial affairs, supply and marketing, sanitation, and medical service departments.

Correctional institutions for juvenile offenders According to Article 21 of the Reform Through Labor Regulations and Article 14 of the Criminal Law, correctional institutions for juvenile offenders are to educate, redeem and reform law offenders who are fourteen to seventeen of age.

GUIDING PRINCIPLE FOR
THE WORK OF LABOR REFORM

"Reform first, production second" is the basic guiding principle for China's reform through labor process. Over the past three decades and more, China has achieved great successes in its reform through labor work under the guidance of this principle. It succeeded in reforming the last emperor of the Qing Dynasty, Japanese war criminals, war criminals of the puppet state of Manchukuo, war criminals of the Chiang Kai-shek clique, and large numbers of counterrevolutionaries, not to mention common criminals. China will continue to uphold this principle so as to guide its efforts at criminal rehabilitation through labor. To gain a general understanding of China's innovations in reform, it is necessary to study the contents and characteristics of its guiding principle for reform through labor.

Formulation of the guiding principle In the early years since 1949, among the social dross left over from the old society, there were a large number of criminals who needed to be imprisoned and punished. But there were not enough prisons. To solve this problem, to educate them, and to let them earn their own living, the institutions of justice organized the criminals to build water conservation projects, roads and houses, and land reclamation as well as other productive activities, while giving them ideological education. This practice was institutionalized in law through the Reform Through Labor Regulations of the People's Republic of China promulgated by the State Council on August 20, 1954. The regulations provide: "In carrying out the reform of counterrevolutionaries and other criminals, the reform through labor institutions should follow the principle of combining punitive control with ideological remolding, and productive labor with political education." Between the second half of 1955 and early 1956, the Chinese Government, in view of the fact that some labor reform institutions emphasized productive labor to the neglect of ideological remolding of criminals, put forth the guiding principle for the country's labor reform: "Reform first, production second." This principle was confirmed formally by the National Conference on the Work of Labor Reform in 1964.

161

Basic content of the guiding principle By "Reform first, production second," primary focus is given to the political objective of remolding criminals into new people, while making secondary the economic benefits derived from their labor. During the period in which China was placing primary emphasis on economic construction, criminals were organized to engage in productive labor. Consequently, there often appeared fairly sharp contradictions between political and economic tasks, and reform and production. The question was whether primary focus should be given to reform or to production, and whether greater importance attached to education of criminals or to economic benefits derived from their labor. The principle of "Reform first, production second" not only pinpointed the main contradictions in the work of labor reform, but also clarified the close relationship between reform and production in which reform is the primary goal and production is in service of reform. Here, "Reform first" covers not only the political aim of reforming criminals, but also involves different kinds of reform measures such as punitive control, political and ideological education, learning of general knowledge, and exposure to scientific and technological knowledge as well as personal and moral hygiene. " Production second" refers to production tasks and economic benefits, including production planning, product quality, and profits.

The guiding principle The guiding principle embodies the role of reform played by criminal punishment in China. Specific provisions concerning the reform of convicted counter-revolutionaries and all other criminals through labor can be found in the Constitution, the Criminal Law and the Reform Through Labor Regulations. Article 1 of the Reform Through Labor Regulations provides: "These regulations are formulated in accordance with the provisions of Article 7 in the Common Program of the Chinese National People's Consultative Conference in order to punish all counterrevolutionaries and other criminals, to force them to remold themselves and become new people in the course of productive labor."

Articles 41 and 43 of the Criminal Law adopted in 1979 stipulate that reform through labor shall be carried out on criminals sentenced to fixed term imprisonment, life imprisonment, or the death penalty with a two-year stay of execution. Article

28 of the 1982 Constitution provides: "The state maintains public order and suppresses treasonable and counterrevolutionary activities. It penalizes actions that endanger public security and disrupt the socialist economy and other criminal activities; and it punishes and reforms criminals."

To punish and reform criminals by placing emphasis on reform is an important feature of China's socialist criminal rehabilitation system. International trends in criminal rehabilitation show a gradual reduction in criminal punishment as societies become more humane. The Chinese criminal justice system also reflects these developments. An important question is the role of criminal punishment in reform and rehabilitation. A fundamental requirement of China's criminal punishment is the reform of criminals into productive and law-abiding citizens in a socialist state: The principle "Reform first, production second" specifically embodies this requirement in its components:

—It is believed that the majority of criminals can be reformed;

—Criminal punishment is an indispensable prerequisite for reform;

—Supervision and control of criminals are necessary for smooth progression in labor reform;

—Reform through labor and reform through education are basic channels for criminals to mend their ways and turn over a new leaf;

— Educating criminals in general, scientific, and technological knowledge, and production skills can ensure the quality of reform;

— The ideology that production is subordinate to, and serves, the political aim of reforming criminals is upheld;

—Production management should be scientific and modern, with a focus on the nature and characteristics of forced labor, to encourage criminals to become better workers;

—Contradictions between reform and production must be resolved in favor of reform; and

—All functional departments of production and reform in prisons and reform through labor teams must emphasize remolding the ideology of criminals while ensuring successful completion of production tasks.

CONTENTS AND PRINCIPLES OF
EDUCATION AND REFORM

China's reform through labor institutions are schools for remolding the ideology of criminals through special education. This special education is designed to transform the ideology of criminals and re-educate them. To rid them of their corrupt, degenerate, and selfish habits in violation of socialist ethics, meticulous ideological education must be given to criminals to help them change their erroneous modes of thinking. Through ideological education, they are encouraged to reform and become new, law-abiding citizens, supporting the socialist system and socialist ethics. This objective can only be achieved by concurrent re-education in general knowledge, and scientific and technological production skills. Only by this two-prong re-education program can criminals be given the assistance they need to adopt the correct attitude toward labor and have the skills necessary for their employment or continued schooling after completing their sentences.

At present, juvenile delinquents make up a rather high percentage of offenders. As criminals, they harmed others, but at the same time, they are victims as well. In educating and reforming them, the state should treat them as children who have become "ill," diagnose their "illness" with care and prescribe the best treatment possible. Great concern should be shown for their lives, studies, labor and reform. By meticulous ideological work, reform institutions can educate and enlighten these delinquents to bring about a desire within them to reform and turn over a new leaf.

Contents of education Education includes political, cultural and technical education. Political education is a key link in transforming criminal ideology and correcting bad habits. Political education involves education in the four cardinal principles, [1] in the socialist legal system, in socialist ethics and outlook, and in the present situation and policies.

---

[1] They are: keeping to the socialist road, upholding the people's democratic dictatorship, upholding the leadership of the Communist Party, and upholding Marxism–Leninism and Mao Zedong Thought.

Cultural education is general education and scientific knowledge. It includes the teaching of language, mathematics, history, geography, physics, chemistry, biology, and other subjects. Different classes should be set up according to the actual educational level of criminals: literacy class, elementary education, junior high school education class, and a self-teaching group for certain university courses.

Literacy class, attended by illiterates and semi-literates who are at the age of 50 or less, offers language and mathematics. The class teaches its students to read and write twenty to twenty-five hundred Chinese characters within two to three years, read newspapers, write simple letters, do calculations of round figures and four decimals, and calculate by abacus. The class of elementary education, mainly attended by people at the age of forty-five or less with an education equivalent to grade four or five of elementary school, offers studies in Chinese language, mathematics and general knowledge of the natural world. It requires its participants to acquire the education level of primary school graduates. The class of junior high school education mainly recruits criminals who are at the age of forty or less, and have a primary school education. It offers studies in Chinese language, mathematics, physics, chemistry, biology, history and geography. It may also offer foreign language studies if conditions permit. Those with a junior high school education may be organized to study senior high school courses, and those with a senior high school is an education are encouraged to study courses from a correspondence university or TV university. Technical education refers to education in production skills.

In the light of different jobs available to criminals, and their different cultural and technical levels, there is an elementary technical class, a middle technical class and a comprehensive technical class, all of which offer technical training. The elementary technical class mainly recruits new criminals and those with only junior high school education or less, offering basic knowledge in production.

The class teaches the criminals what skills are required by present production and follows the principle of "Smaller quantity, better quality" in its approach. With regard to those who are engaged in farm production, the class focuses on crop cultiva-

165

tion, the breeding of fine strains, soil and fertilizer, irrigation and water conservation, animal and plant protection, diseases and pests prevention, repair and maintenance of farm tools, and management of crops. Those engaged in forestry, animal husbandry, industrial and sideline production are offered knowledge on tree-planting, livestock breeding, horticulture, breeding of aquatic products, and the processing of farm and sideline products.

Those criminals engaged in industrial production primarily study basic knowledge of their own trades, and knowledge of their technological processes, operations and safety regulations. Through studies and training, they are required to master the basic knowledge so as to be familiar with the structure of the equipment they use, the methods of machine repair and maintenance, reaching the level of a primary worker within three years. The middle technical class mainly recruits those with a junior high school education and at the age of thirty-five or less. The pupils are required to master the basic theory and operational skills of their specific jobs within three to five years and to attain the level of an average worker. The comprehensive technical class organizes those criminals not engaged in technical production to learn vocational and handicraft skills, including the art of cooking, tailoring, hair-cutting, carpentry, brick-laying, electrical engineering, repair and maintenance of machines.

Principles and methods of education The principles of education are the basic criteria by which China's reform through labor institutions educate and reform criminals. The major principles are integrating theory with practice, educating criminals in accordance with their specific conditions, and persuasion by reason.

The principle of combining theory with practice requires that education applied to criminals be factual. It also demands that labor reform personnel match their words with actions, and set good examples.

The principle of educating criminals according to their specific conditions requires that appropriate education contents and methods be employed. Criminals will therefore be educated in the light of the nature and causes of their crimes, and in accordance with their education level, personal experience, as well as their ideology and behavior.

The principle of persuasion by reason requires the presentation of facts and reason in analyzing and solving criminals' problems. Sophistry and abuse of power should be avoided. Persuasion by reason allows criminals to set forth their arguments and viewpoints, and speak their minds so they can be educated and reformed according to their individual needs. For instance, before educating a criminal individually, we should get to know his situation as a whole, his ideological problems and personal characteristics, so as to find a suitable educational method. Advance investigation should be made in dealing with the problems of reforming criminals so as to avoid further contradictions. When a problem arises, its solution can only be arrived at by patient clarification of the facts and discussion with the criminal concerned so right can be distinguished from wrong. This approach gives the criminal some flexibility and makes his acceptance of criticism easier.

Educational methods are very important for educating and reforming criminals. China's labor reform institutions generally employ the following educational methods: a combination of collective education and individual education, a combination of rational education and perceptual education, and a combination of prison and social education. Based on common problems of criminals, collective education employs the methods of general education, such as lectures, group discussions, report meetings, seminars, training courses, exhibitions, social visits, reports given by well-known public figures or by family members of criminals, and a selection of activists.

Individual education is based on the special problems of individual criminals with discussion as the main form. A combination of rational and perceptual education means that reform and education of criminals by labor reform institutions should be based on the law of humane cognition and apply a vivid and specific education in image projection. For instance, labor reform personnel should set an example in observing discipline and in fostering lofty ideals and ethics, thus giving criminals a perceptual education. Earnest efforts should be made to strictly enforce discipline, follow good hygiene both inside and outside their rooms, promote socialist ethics and civil behavior, improve

167

the diet of criminals, cure the sick and invalid and reward those who have made progress. All these are facets of perpetual education. Great attention should be paid to rational education to enhance the criminals' theoretical understanding of the importance and necessity of active reform and education. A combination of prison and social education has proved very effective in reforming criminals. While carrying out prison education, labor reform institutions should rely on different social sectors in a selective manner so as to conduct social education on criminals. This serves to consolidate, broaden and enrich education carried out in prison.

Methods of this kind are many. For instance, in regard to certain criminals who refuse to admit their guilt, we may let them meet their family members, or invite leaders of the organizations of the victims, or those who know the situation intimately to come to the prison and help educate them. We may also organize some visits outside prison or invite some ex-criminals who have made remarkable contributions to the society to come to the prison to talk about their experiences. We may also carry out auxiliary education, such as sports and recreational activities to help transform them positively.

The first and last lesson of criminals in prison Upon their arrival in prison, criminals are given their first lesson on education and reform. The major objectives of the first lesson are to publicize and explain state laws and decrees, the guiding principles underlying reform through labor and to remove their anxieties and suspicions. These steps are necessary to enable criminals to accept punishment and undergo reform through labor. Criminals are required to do the following during their reformation:

—Abide by state laws, love the motherland, strictly observe prison regulations and disciplines;

—Obey labor reform personnel and do not go beyond designated security lines and activity areas;

—Earnestly study politics, general knowledge and scientific and technological knowledge;

— Take an active part in productive labor, observe operational regulations, ensure product quality, and complete production tasks;

—Strictly observe the sanitation system, work and rest according to a timetable, keep rooms clean and tidy, and maintain personal and environmental hygiene;

— Never resist labor or stay away from studies while continually guarding against the formation of gangs or cliques, fighting, perpetrating in-prison crimes or instigating others to commit crimes; and

—Pay attention to polite and civil behavior, observe social ethics and discipline, and foster socialist social conduct.

Should anyone violate any of the above requirements, he will be criticized or even punished. Those who have consistently behaved well, or particularly well, will be rewarded. Through their first lesson in prison, criminals are enabled to understand what they should and should not do, so as to lay a good foundation for their shifting from forced to conscious reform.

China's prisons and labor reform teams generally organize criminals to review and consolidate progress achieved through reform and education one month prior to their completion of sentence. This is to make ample preparation for the rehabilitation of a criminal going back into society. The contents of education conducted in this period should cover education in the current situation, state policies and the legal system, correct attitude toward employment and personal ideals and prospects. The method should be a combination of collective and individual education with an emphasis on individual education. During this period of education, criminals may be assigned light work and labor, and control over them may be relaxed appropriately.

CHAPTER *12*

Notary System

The notary system is part of China's judicial system as well as a component part of its legal system. In China, notary institutions are established by the state and notaries are state personnel. China's notary activities are aimed at protecting the interests of the state and the rights and interests of its citizens. The tasks of the notary institutions are to protect public property, to safeguard the legitimate rights and interests of state institutions, enterprises and social organizations, to guarantee the legitimate rights and interests of the citizens regarding their status and property, to reduce the number of disputes and public prosecutions, to strengthen social stability and unity, and to improve and consolidate the socialist legal system. The end result should be the promotion of the smooth progress of the socialist modernization drive.

China's notary work began in the mid-1940s. Over the past three decades, the notary system has gone through a cyclical process of development, decline, stagnation, rebuilding and again development. On April 12, 1982, the Provisional Regulations Regarding Public Notary of the People's Republic of China were promulgated by the State Council, consisting of six chapters and thirty articles. The regulations have designated the organizational structure of China's notary institutions, the nature of the notary system and the scope of service of the notary institutions, the procedures and guiding principle of handling public notaries, the effect of notarial deeds and the jurisdictions of notary institutions. The promulgation and implementation of these regulations signal that China's notary system has matured and is entering a new stage of development. The regulations have summed up several decades of practical experience with notary publics, and have legally provided for the organizational structure of the notary system, its principles and methods of work, as well as its scope of service. These regulations constitute the basic guidelines for China's notary services and are key documents in the understanding of the country's notary system.

ESTABLISHMENT AND DEVELOPMENT OF CHINA'S NOTARY SYSTEM

There existed many years ago in Chinese history the practice of having a middleman as a witness. Contracts were signed when major rights and interests were involved, such as inheritance, buying or selling land and houses, or extending loans. Back in 1935, the Kuomintang regime promulgated the Provisional Regulations Regarding Public Notary, but never put them into effect.

The notary work of the People's Republic began even before its founding, in the period 1946-1949, in big cities like Harbin, Shenyang and Shanghai along with the establishment of the people's power. Meeting the conditions and needs of the time, notary services mainly involved notarization of marriage, divorce, child adoption, certification of appointments, and contracts. They played a role in safeguarding the legal rights and interests of citizens in regards to status and property.

In the early days of the People's Republic, China needed reconstruction. Its most urgent task was to heal the wounds of war and to revive and develop the national economy. Like its judicial system, China's notary system provided services for the development of the socialist economy, transformation of the capitalist industry and commerce, and for the protection of public properties. During this period, the people's courts in the cities provided notarial deeds for economic contracts signed between state institutions and state-owned enterprises on one hand, and private industrial and commercial enterprises on the other. These contracts concerned processing, placing orders, handling distribution, or distribution on a commission basis on behalf of state trading concerns or cooperatives. In 1956 alone, the notary institutions handled more than 224,000 cases, of which over ninety percent were certifications of economic contracts.

Notarization of economic contracts effectively guaranteed the supervision and transformation of capitalist industry and commerce in the economic sphere, and promoted progress in the socialist economy. Meanwhile, the notary system witnessed great development.

In a report to the State Council, the Ministry of Justice made, in principle, the following decisions: notary departments were to be established in municipalities directly under the Central Government, and cities with a population of three hundred thousand people and above; notary sections should be established under the people's courts of the cities and counties that had a population of less than three hundred thousand, but with a large number of family dependants or relatives of Chinese nationals residing abroad. By the end of 1957, fifty-two cities had established notary departments, and 553 city or county people's courts had established affiliated notary sections; judges of 625 county people's courts also provided notary services. With the increasing number of notary institutions and development of notary services, notary procedure had become more formal. The Ministry of Justice held two national conferences on notary public, drafted " notary regulations" and promulgated uniform "written notary forms," "rates of notary fees, and management of notary funds." As a result, great progress was made in developing notary services. Practice showed that the notary system was a good one. But owing to the influence of the " Left" deviationist trend of thought on judicial work, some people held that notarization of economic contracts had completed its historical mission. Since Communist ideology had been greatly popularized and there no longer existed civil legal problems involving private properties, they argued, it was no longer necessary to provide notary services for guaranteeing rights, interests, and obligations of citizens. Under this erroneous influence, almost all of China's notary institutions were dismantled, except for people's courts in a few big cities still providing some foreign notary services according to customary international practice.

Throughout the chaotic decade, the socialist legal system

was seriously disrupted. Notary service was condemned as a " revisionist system," while foreign notary service was condemned for "giving a green light to having illicit relations with foreign countries." In those years, even Shanghai, Tianjin and Guangzhou, which in the past had possessed a large volume of notary services, handled only several dozen cases annually.

Since the historical meeting of 1978, China's notary services have been rapidly rehabilitated and developed. In February 1980, the Ministry of Justice issued a Circula on Gradual Rehabilitation of Domestic Notary Services, calling for the first application of domestic notary services to such cases as the notarization of adopted children, wills, bequests, entrustment, and endowments, so as to meet the needs of citizens.

In March of the same year, the Ministry of Justice issued the Circular on the Establishment and Management of the System of Notary Departments. According to the circular, notary departments are to be established in the municipalities directly under the Central Government, the cities directly under the provincial authorities and counties.

In those cities and counties where notary sections are not to be established, local people's courts shall have their notaries or judges provide notary services concurrently. In September 1980, the Ministry of Justice held a national forum on notary work. The forum discussed the principle, tasks and organizational building of the notary system, thus unifying people's thinking and understanding.

Meanwhile, the Ministry of Justice drafted the Provisional Regulations Regarding Public Notary of the People's Republic of China. The State Council promulgated these regulations in April 1982. As China's first notary regulations, they summarized the country's many years of notary experiences, thus establishing a fairly complete notary system.

The promulgation and implementation of the provisional notary regulations have brought great progress in China's notary services. The past few years have been the best period for the country's notary services with well over a million cases a year. China's notary public focuses on promoting and safeguarding the socialist modernization drive with economic development as the emphasis. Notarization of economic contracts constitutes the

173

main emphasis of the country's notary services and a legal approach to managing the economy.

As practice shows, examination of economic contracts helps prevent counterfeit and illegal contracts, and exposes such illegalities as deception, speculation, and profiteering. By protecting state property and collective interests, notarization has been warmly received by legal persons and citizens. Notary work in the rural areas over the past two years has focused on notarization of specialized contracts based on contracted responsibilities, or of individual partnerships and joint ventures, promoting the development of rural commodity economy.

Since the implementation of the open door policy, with steady increase of foreign economic exchanges, state institutions, enterprises and other organizations have demanded more foreign notary services. To meet the growing needs of certain organizations in promoting foreign business, such as tendering or securing loans, contracting engineering projects, providing labor services, promoting the sales of products and the importation of advanced equipment, as well as the needs of public prosecutions, the notary institutions provide over eighty kinds of notary services. These include the notarization of authorization documents, agreements, statements, labor insurance certificates, business licenses, and certificates of mutual benefit. Providing these notary services for Chinese legal persons has protected and promoted China's economic exchanges with other countries.

ORGANIZATION AND SERVICES PROVIDED BY NOTARIES

A component part of its judicial system, China's notary system is of a socialist nature. It has unique features in regard to its organizations, system of management, principles guiding its services, and the people it serves. For example, the organizations that exercise notarial functions are state institutions; notary institutions are staffed by state personnel; and notary institutions and concerned parties have no direct monetary relationship. In China, notary institutions charge very low fees in providing notary services, and deliver all revenue to the state treasury. The operating expenses of the notary institutions and the salaries of their personnel are covered under state budget.

In China, all notary services shall take facts as the basis and law as the criterion. They are directed at protecting public property and the legitimate rights and interests of citizens. Article 2 of the Provisional Regulations Regarding Public Notary provides that "State notary institutions are to certify upon application of the parties concerned and according to law, the legal acts, documents with legal significance, and truth and legality of facts, so as to protect public properties and the legal rights and interests of citizens regarding their status and properties." The socialist nature and characteristics of China's notary system are embodied in the organizational structure of the notary institutions and the scope of notary services.

The organizational structure of notary institutions and their system of management According to the Provisional Regulations Regarding Public Notary, notary institutions are state institutions. They may be established in cities directly under the provincial government, counties (including autonomous counties) and cities, with the approval of the administrative institutions of justice of the provinces, autonomous regions and municipalities directly under the Central Government. Notary institutions are independent from each other and have the same effect. Notary institutions are led and supervised by the administrative institutions of justice at the corresponding level and at the higher level. The Ministry of Justice exercises its leadership over the notary institutions in the country through the judicial administrative institutions at different levels.

Personnel of the notary institutions include notaries and assistant notaries. According to their needs, they may have a director and a deputy-director. The directorship and deputy directorship should be taken up by notaries while functioning as notaries at the same time. Directors, deputy-directors, notaries, and assistant notaries are appointed and dismissed from office by the people's governments of cities directly under the provincial government, and of counties and cities according to personnel management regulations. According to the Provisional Regulations Regarding Public Notary, citizens who have the right to vote and to be elected, and who also meet one of the following conditions, may be appointed as notaries:

— College law graduates who have engaged in judicial work, legal teaching or research for at least one year;

—Those who have served as judges in a people's court or as procurators of a people's procuratorate; and

—Those who have engaged in judicial work within judicial administrative institutions for two years and more, or those who have worked in other state institutions, people's organizations, enterprises or institutions for five years or longer, and have acquired the legal knowledge of a middle law school graduate. According to Article 9 of the Provisional Regulations Regarding Public Notary, law college graduates who have completed their probational period, or those state personnel who have the equivalent educational level, may be appointed assistant notaries.

Notary services According to the provisional regulations, notary institutions shall provide the following services:

— Notarization of contracts, appointments, wills or bequests;

—Notarization of inheritance rights;

—Notarization of donation and division of properties;

—Notarization of child adoption;

—Notarization of kinfolk relationships;

— Notarization of status, education, and personal experience;

— Notarization of birthdates, marriage status, birth and death;

—Notarization of the signature and seal in the document;

—Notarization of the authenticity of copies, abridged editions, translations and photocopies of the original;

— Notarization of the compulsory implementation of the documents in pursuance of loans and materials;

—Preservation of evidence;

—Custody of wills and other documents;

—Drafting application for notary service on behalf of concerned parties; and

—Providing other notary services upon application of concerned parties and according to customary international practice.

The above fourteen items roughly fall into the following

176

four categories:

Certification of legal acts Acts which cause the establishment, change and termination of civil rights and obligations are known as legal acts. In everyday social life, some legal acts involve fairly important matters, such as signing of contracts, adoption of a child, and buying or selling of a house. There should be written documents with notarization by notary institutions to avoid possible future disputes. They also provide legal supervision over the concerned parties to urge them to carry out their duties faithfully. These types of notarizations constitute a fairly high ratio of the cases handled by China's notary institutions. Many of them are economic contracts between legal persons and other legal persons, and between citizens. As China proceeds in its economic reconstruction and further opens to the outside world, this type of notarization will become even more important.

Notarization of documents with legal significance Documents with legal significance refer to those other than documents of legal acts. Notaries certify educational documents and personal documents. They also serve organizations issuing driver's licenses with certifying the signatures and seals of their leading members. In addition, they also certify the authenticity of copies, abridged versions with the original documents, and the authenticity of translations with the original. All documents with legal significance, except confidential ones, issued by state institutions, people's organizations, and enterprises and institutions, may be notarized upon application of the concerned parties.

Notarization of legal facts Legal facts refer to those of natural occurrence and existence, such as birth, death, the existence or the disappearance of a person, and the occurrence of a disaster. In China, certain rights and obligations of concerned parties are often determined in the light of the occurrence, existence and elimination of these legally significant facts.

Under these circumstances, it is necessary to certify the existence of these facts so that the concerned parties will enjoy certain rights and undertake their obligations. For instance, an overseas Chinese died within the territory of China and left behind certain property in a foreign country. If his or her children wanted to inherit his property, customary international practice and the requirements of the country concerned demand that a Chinese notary institution notarize the death of the person and the relationship between the deceased and the beneficiary, so that the beneficiary can begin the procedures of inheritance. In this regard, China's notary institutions certify death, existence, nationality, citizenship, kinfolk relationship, disappearance and *force majeure*.

Handling auxiliary work Auxiliary work involves taking custody of documents of value, evidence and other documents. It also includes drafting of other legal documents such as contracts, certificates of delegation and statements. Although these matters do not require actual certification, they are related to notary services and, therefore, fall into this category of auxiliary services.

PROCEDURE AND PRINCIPLES OF NOTARY SERVICES

The Provisional Regulations Regarding Public Notary of the People's Republic of China outline in a special chapter the procedure of notary service. It may be summarized as follows:

Applying for notarization Citizens, legal persons, or their legal representatives fill out different forms of applications for notary services depending on the notarization items. They may also file their applications in written or oral form. Oral applications should be written down by notaries for the record. A person entrusted to file such an application should present a letter of delegation. When an authorized representative of a legal person applies for notary service, he should present a certificate of authorization. Apart from providing certificates to verify their status, the legal representatives should present relevant certificates regarding the facts and matters to be handled. In applications for the notarization of delegation, child adoption, wills and bequests, the signature and seal should be made by the concerned parties.

Investigation and examination

Examining the parties Notary services examine and investigate applicants to ensure they are proper parties able to exercise their rights and perform their obligations. In examining the capability of state institutions, enterprises, institutions and social organizations as legal entities in the performance of legal duties, notary institutions must look into whether these entities perform their duties in accordance with the intent and purpose of the applicable legal act.

Examining notarization items Notaries examine the truth and legality of the notarization items filed by applicants, as well as their relevant papers and documents. If the notarization items are not true to the facts and do not accord with state laws and decrees, notary institutions shall deny notarization even if the parties have the ability to exercise their rights and perform their obligations. Evidence to be examined include statements of the parties, testimony of witnesses, and written evidence. Evidence provided by the parties, when considered incomplete or unclear, may be supplemented as suggested by notary institutions. Notary institutions have the right to make investigations and acquire evidence and relevant documents from relevant departments. In regard to technical problems, opinions should be sought from relevant departments. If notary institutions discover in their examination of notarization items any acts avoiding legal liability, endangering the state's interests, and encroaching upon the legitimate rights and interests of third parties, they have the right to expose such acts.

Granting notarial deeds Generally speaking, notarial deeds should be given with regard to all items for notarization if they are found to conform to notary regulations. Notarial deeds should bear the statement that the items for notarization are found to be true to the facts, along with the name of the notary institution, serial number of the document, the date of handling, the signature or seal of the notary, and the seal of the notary institution.

Public notary in China is a certification activity carried out by notaries on behalf of the state. Such certification should be serious, earnest, meticulous and accurate. To guard against errors, Chinese notary institutions require notaries to abide by the following principles in handling notary services.

The legal principle All notary activities should take facts as the basis and law as the criterion, and emphasize the trustfulness and legality of the notary items. Notaries should ensure that the notarial deeds they issue conform to state legal provisions, both in form and in content. Notaries should refuse untrue and illegal notarial items, and expose acts of deception and counterfeiting of documents.

The principle of recusal Recusal is a Chinese legal provision observed by judicial institutions in carrying out criminal and civil procedures. Recusal means judicial personnel do not get involved in handling cases in which they have an interest or other relationship. The aim of recusal is to avoid suspicion and guard against abusing one's position to seek personal gains. The personnel of the notary institutions should also abide by this principle of recusal in providing notary services. To guarantee that the notarization is fair and objective, the Provisional Regulations Regarding Public Notary provide that notary personnel do not become involved in providing notary services to their spouses, their relatives and relatives of their spouses, nor do they handle cases that they or their spouses may have an interest. A party concerned has the right to request the recusal of a member of the notary personnel.

The principle of confidentiality All personnel of the notary institutions should keep confidential all notary services they provide. All notarial documents must be taken good care of to avoid loss or breach of confidentiality. Under normal circumstances, notarial deeds shall be granted only to parties who apply for notary services or to their agents. Several copies may be given to the parties depending on their needs. This principle is upheld by Chinese notary institutions in protecting the legal rights and interests of the parties.

The principle of helping the people In providing notary services, Chinese notary institutions adopt methods and procedure aimed at helping the people. Their notarial procedure is simple, swift and timely, and no additional conditions can be attached other than procedure prescribed in the provisional regulations. Regarding notarial deeds to be used abroad, Chinese notary institutions place special emphasis on their timeliness. Notarial items with clear facts and complete evidence should be handled readily. Notarial personnel may go to areas where many people apply for notary services, and they may deliver door-to-door services to those applicants who are sick or live far away from notary institutions. Notary cases which are incomplete and which need supplemented materials from the parties or further investigation by notary institutions should also be handled as soon as possible.

The principle of voluntariness Application of notarial services by parties is a right and not an obligation. Except for those documents that must be notarized according to law, it is entirely up to the parties to decide whether or not to apply for notarial services for their legal actions, legal facts and documents with legal significance according to their needs.

EFFECTIVENESS OF NOTARIAL DEEDS AND JURISDICTIONS OF CHINA'S NOTARY INSTITUTIONS

At present, Chinese law has no specified provisions pertaining to the legal effectiveness of legal acts, legal facts and documents with legal significance notarized by Chinese notary institutions. Among jurists opinions differ but the majority consider notarial deeds to have legal effect, evidentiary effect and executory effect.

Evidentiary effect All notarial deeds provided by notary institutions have evidentiary effect and therefore have the legal force of evidence. Article 59 of the Provisional Civil Procedure Law of the People's Republic of China provides that "People's courts should recognize the legal effectiveness of notarized legal acts, legal facts and documents except where sufficient evidence proves to the contrary."

Effect of compulsory execution Such effect of notarial deeds refers to the right to pursue indisputable loans and materials, and it does not mean that all notarial deeds possess such effect. Paragraph 10 of Article 4 of the Provisional Regulations Regarding Public Notary specifies that "Documents pursuing loans and materials which are considered indisputable can be certified to possess the effect for compulsory execution."

Legal effect Such effect refers to legal acts that should be notarized according to law or the agreement of the parties. Legal acts that fail to go through notarial procedure do not have legal effect, i.e., notarized legal acts possess legal effect. Therefore notarization is one of the conditions for making a legal act effective. China's present laws and decrees do not provide for specified legal acts that must be notarized. However, if the parties agree that a certain legal act must be notarized, notarization then becomes one of the necessary conditions for making the act in question legally effective. So documents notarized under these circumstances possess legal effect. As for documents to be sent to foreign countries by Chinese legal persons or citizens, they must first be notarized according to customary international practice, then submitted to the Chinese foreign affairs departments or foreign embassies or consulates in China for certification. Only by going through this procedure can they have legal effects in foreign countries.

China's notary institutions have their own scope of jurisdiction. The major jurisdictions include regional jurisdiction, designated jurisdiction, and special jurisdiction.

Regional jurisdiction In China, notarial affairs are mostly handled by notary institutions in the areas where the parties have their registered residence or where legal acts or facts occurred. Notarial affairs involving property transfer are handled by notary institutions in the areas where the parties have their registered residence or where the major properties are located. If the parties applying for notarial services do not belong to the same notarial jurisdiction area or their properties belong to several notarial jurisdictions, they may agree to file their application in one of the notarial jurisdictions. If the parties fail to reach an agreement, the relevant notary institutions may decide which, among them, may accept the application for notarial services.

Designated jurisdiction Should there be any dispute between notary institutions in regard to their jurisdiction, the judicial administrative institution at the higher level shall be responsible for designating jurisdiction for them. In other words, the Ministry of Justice and the judicial administrative departments (or bureaus) of the provinces, municipalities directly under the Central Government and the autonomous regions have the right to designate certain notarial services for notary institutions at lower levels.

Special jurisdiction When notary institutions are unable to perform their notarial functions in special situations, certain special departments may, according to provisions of law, act as proxies to perform notarial services. The notarial deeds they issue shall possess the same effect as those issued by the notary institutions. In the light of China's experiences in notarial practice and customary international practice, certain notarial services may be performed by the following departments as proxies of notary institutions. For instance, Chinese embassies and consulates in foreign countries provide certain notarial services so as to protect the legitimate rights and interests of Chinese citizens and legal persons. In addition, the following certificates have the same effect as those issued by notary institutions: inspection certificates issued by import and export commodity inspection agencies and certified by the supervisor of the foreign trade agencies; immunity certificates, health certificates, death certificates, and birth certificates issued by health departments; certificates issued by captains of the aircraft and vessels of wills or documents of delegation written by citizens aboard the aircraft or the ship; certificates issued by leaders of prospecting and exploring teams and other field work teams of wills and documents of delegation written by their team members during their field work; certificates issued by leaders of places in which no freedom of action is allowed of wills or documents of delegation written by people living under these circumstances.

CHAPTER 13

Attorney System

China's attorney system is a legal structure under which state-recognized, qualified lawyers provide the state, communities, and individual citizens with legal assistance in defense of their legitimate rights and interests. It plays an extremely important role in further enhancing China's democratic process, perfecting the legal system, and promoting the modernization drive. China's attorney system is a component of its judicial system. Compared with the attorney system of the Western countries, it contains uniquely Chinese characteristics.

Based on socialist public ownership, the attorney system serves the socialist economy and society. China's lawyers are state personnel who specialize in legal affairs. They are different from their counterparts in the Western countries. The work units of China's lawyers are accountable to the unified leadership, supervision and management of state justice administrative institutions. They practice within a collective work system and in this respect, they are quite different from law offices freely operated in the West.

China's attorneys are only in a position to help parties through their professional knowledge. They are not allowed to direct public prosecutions. The Provisional Regulations Regarding Lawyers of the People's Republic of China, promulgated in 1980, provides the legal structure for the country's attorney system. Consisting of four chapters with twenty-one articles, the regulations designate the tasks and rights of lawyers, as well as their qualifications to practice, and the work organizations within which they will function. This document is basic to an understanding of China's attorney system.

ESTABLISHMENT AND GROWTH

The attorney system of the People's Republic was gradually established following the abolition of the old system in 1950. The First National Conference on Judicial Work in 1950 suggested the abolition of the old attorney system, and the establishment of a new one. The Ministry of Justice decided in 1954 that Beijing, Shanghai, Tianjin, Chongqing, Shenyang and other big cities should operate their own law offices on an experimental basis. The Constitution and the Organic Law of the People's Courts, promulgated in 1955, clearly designate China's attorney system. In 1956, the Ministry of Justice held a national forum on judicial practice by lawyers. The forum clearly outlined both the guiding principles, and the tasks and scope of services rendered by lawyers. The forum concluded that legal consultation offices staffed with a number of lawyers shall be established in large and medium-sized cities with a population of three hundred thousand or more, and in cities and counties where higher and intermediate people's courts had already been established. In July 1956, the State Council approved the Report on the Establishment of Law Offices submitted by the Ministry of Justice and promulgated the Provisional Regulations on Counsel Fees, thus promoting greatly the development of the country's legal services. By June 1957, China had established nineteen lawyers associations at provincial and municipal levels, and had over eight hundred legal consultants, and more than twenty-five hundred lawyers. This was an important factor for strengthening the country's legal system. Not long after, however, China's newly established attorney system was wrongly criticized because of erroneous "Leftist" ideologies which broadened the scope of the Anti-Rightist Movement in 1957. This resulted in the destruction of the two-year-old attorney system.

After the smashing of the Lin Biao and Jiang Qing counterrevolutionary cliques, and especially since the Third Plenary Session in 1978, the CPC and government attached great importance to extending legal services throughout the country. Deng Xiaoping, Chairman of the Central Military Commission, pointed out in 1980 that "Enterprises should employ lawyers as their legal consultants and China's contingent of lawyers should be expanded. It will not do without the attorney system." The Fifth NPC Standing Committee adopted, at its Fifteenth Session on August 20, 1980, the Provisional Regulations Regarding Lawyers of the People's Republic of China. The promulgation and implementation of the provisional regulations brought about a new stage of development for the country's attorney system. In October 1980, the Ministry of Justice held a national forum on legal services. The forum further clarified the tasks and orientation of lawyers and came to an understanding that lawyers should serve the country's economic construction. This boosted the development of the attorney system and laid a solid foundation for its all-round growth.

Progress has been made over the past few years both in developing the contingent of lawyers and their services. The scope of legal services has been broadened and the number of attorneys increasing steadily. China now has full-time lawyers, part-time lawyers and specially invited lawyers. The number of China's law offices is also increasing. There are now not only general law offices, but specialized ones handling economic affairs, foreign economic relations, overseas Chinese affairs, maritime issues, and patents. It now has more than thirty-one hundred law offices and over twenty thousand full-time lawyers, part-time lawyers and legal personnel. More than twenty thousand enterprises have employed lawyers as their legal advisors. According to statistics of the past six years, lawyers acted as defenders in 530,000 criminal cases by court appointment or retained by the concerned parties, provided legal representation in over 230,000 civil cases, received 940,000 visitors, and handled over five million pieces of legal documents or questions on legal affairs. In the past three years, lawyers have also handled nine hundred thousand economic cases, and have solved thirteen thousand economic disputes on behalf of assigners. In 1985 alone, they handled over fourteen thousand cases on foreign economic affairs, helping both the people's courts with a fair and just application of the law, and protecting the legitimate

186

rights and interests of legal persons and citizens. In addition, lawyers also educate the people in the operation of the socialist legal system and have become an important factor in promoting economic, cultural and ideological progress.

The First National Conference of Representatives of Lawyers was convened in Beijing in July 1983, with the inauguration of the All-China Lawyers Association and the adoption of its twelve-article charter. The conference also elected a fourteen-member standing council. The founding of the All-China Lawyers Association is an important measure for improving and strengthening China's attorney system, with a far-reaching influence on the development of legal services in China. It will also play a significant role in promoting the development of the country's legal system.

TASK OF LAWYERS

The task of China's lawyers is to provide legal persons and citizens with legal assistance so as to guarantee the precise application of law and safeguard the interests of the state, communities, and the legitimate rights and interests of the citizens. This task is achieved by provision of the following legal services:

Serving as legal representatives of enterprises, Party and government institutions, and public organizations Lawyers also serve as legal consultants to industrial and commercial enterprises, to rural contract responsibility households, and to individual partnerships. Moreover, lawyers provide legal services for developing commodity production and exchange, and for promoting economic development. Over the past few years, different aspects of China's economic life have made it increasingly necessary for institutions to avail themselves of legal services, so more and more organizations have employed lawyers as their legal advisors. In 1982, several hundred enterprises employed lawyers as their legal consultants throughout China, but the number has now climbed to over twenty thousand, and is still increasing. In addition, many lawyers have attended foreign economic negotiations or acted as representatives boosting economic policies aimed at building the domestic economy and opening to the outside world. For example, the law office of foreign economic affairs in Shenzhen has, over the past few years, handled several thousand legal cases on foreign economic affairs. This office has played a positive role in safeguarding state sovereignty and economic interests, and in protecting the legitimate rights and interests of foreign businessmen.

Acting as representatives of the litigants in civil matters As a result of China's economic reconstruction and growth of a commodity economy, the number of complex civil cases is increasing and needing more legal assistance. In civil disputes, legal persons and private citizens may appoint a lawyer to act as their representative in mediation. By urging the parties to reach a mutual compromise, attorneys help the courts in resolving disputes through mediation. This emphasis on mediation encourages efficiency in production, promotes stability and unity among people, and creates a harmonious and relaxed environment for economic reconstruction and development. In civil litigation, upon appointment by legal persons and citizens, lawyers can act as their representatives in court. As legal representatives, lawyers must base their work on facts and law, clarify right from wrong, and assist the courts in rendering a fair judgment. Only then are the legal rights and interests of the litigants effectively protected.

Participating in criminal defense work In the 1950s, criminal defense was the principal work of China's lawyers. In 1954, the Ministry of Justice, in its instructions to law offices to be operated experimentally in several large cities, emphasized the importance of lawyers to the application of criminal procedure, as in the holding of public hearings and general defense. Because of the small numbers of lawyers, legal services were generally provided for the most pressing and important matters such as criminal defense. Other legal services provided included responding to legal inquiries and drafting civil complaints on behalf of others. At this time, lawyers seldom acted as representatives for the parties in civil cases.

The trials of Japanese war criminals in the mid-1950s are well-known and far-reaching in impact. In 1956, the Special Military Court of the Supreme People's Court, following the decision of the NPC Standing Committee, put Japanese war criminals Suzuki Keikyu and Buttori Rokuzou on trial. During the trials, Chinese lawyers mounted a vigorous defense, based on law and fact, for the defendants. By providing serious defense to these two war criminals, Chinese defense lawyers played a positive role at home and abroad. Their work had a far-reaching influence in the defense of world peace and in the promotion of friendship between China and Japan.

Defense work in the trial of the Lin Biao and Jiang Qing counterrevolutionary cliques embodied the principle of China's legal system. It was a typical case of criminal defense conducted by Chinese lawyers. According to the decision of the Fifth NPC Standing Committee, the Special Court of the Supreme People's Court put on trial in 1980 ten principal criminals of the Lin Biao and Jiang Qing cliques. In the trial, lawyers undertook the task of defending the criminals. They strictly observed the principle of "Taking facts as the basis and law as the criterion." They clarified facts and applied the law, thus embodying the fundamental principle of the Chinese legal system.

Over the past few years, lawyers in China have participated in cases brought against criminal law offenders and economic law offenders, and have done much of the criminal defense work in cooperation with court hearings. They have gradually worked out a set of legal practices suitable to China's specific conditions and have summarized their experiences.

In criminal defense, lawyers scrupulously follow the law in handling cases. By upholding the principle of "Taking facts as the basis and law as the criterion," they assist the courts in reaching a fair verdict, and guarding against trumped-up cases. In practicing criminal defense, lawyers educate the defendants and encourage them to admit their guilt and obey the law. Often, they even educate the defendant's family members. Through their work, lawyers publicize the legal system. They are an integral part of the comprehensive program against criminality.

Representing parties in informal disputes, mediation, and arbitration In China, parties in informal non-litigation disputes may obtain a lawyer to assist them. Parties may also appoint a lawyer to act as their representative in mediation and arbitration proceedings.

189

In economic disputes, lawyers have mediated and reduced the number of cases litigated. For instance, from 1981 to 1983, lawyers handled thousands of informal non-litigation disputes, thereby fostering unity, stability, and economic development.

Lawyers' participation in arbitration serves economic development directly. The number of non-litigation disputes handled by foreign trade and marine arbitration organizations has risen over the past few years with the further implementation of the open door policy. In many mediation and arbitration activities, lawyers have been invited to participate. By providing legal assistance and encouraging settlement, they help resolve disputes in a timely fashion while protecting the legitimate rights and interests of the parties. These legal services facilitate development in the economy and in international trade.

Responding to legal inquiries and drafting complaints Statistics reveal that annually lawyers receive nearly a million people seeking legal advice, answer a million legal inquiries, and draft thousands of documents. Through these activities, lawyers solve disputes, reduce litigation, and promote unity and stability by de-escalating conflicts. In providing legal services, lawyers disseminate a general knowledge of law and the legal system. Concurrently, the people, by coming into contact with legal services, are further encouraged to study and understand the law and abide by it. This results in growth in China's legal system.

LAWYERS' ORGANIZATIONS

Article 13 of the Provisional Regulations Regarding Lawyers provides that work organizations where lawyers perform their duties are called legal consultation offices. A description of the nature of legal consultation offices as well as their organizational leadership and structure follows.

State institutions China is a socialist country based on the people's democratic dictatorship. Therefore, China's attorney system should serve the socialist economy, should be restrained by socialist public ownership, and should take the organizational form suitable to socialist economic structure. At present, China's lawyers organizations are legal consultation offices, known as law offices. They are non-profit-making state institutions whose revenues are turned over to the Ministry of Finance, and their operating expenses are covered under the state budget.

Legal consultation offices, in principle, are established in counties, cities, and urban districts. They may also be jointly established by the urban districts and municipalities directly under the Central Government, or the urban districts and cities directly under the jurisdiction of the provincial authorities. If necessary, legal consultation offices may also be established in prefectures with approval by the judicial administrative departments of the provinces or autonomous regions. All legal consultation offices are independent from each other. Specialized legal consultation offices may be established with the approval of the Ministry of Justice. To meet the needs of rural economic development, legal consultation stations or judicial administrative offices may be established in the townships or towns to provide legal assistance to rural people.

In China, legal consultation offices correspond, in principle, to the people's courts and people's procuratorates of the same level. They cooperate with and act as a restraint on each other. This helps the people and enables lawyers to go to the grassroots.

Legal consultation offices operate under a unified leadership and supervision. The personnel of a legal consultation office may consist of a few lawyers, financial accountants, typists, orderlies, a chief and a deputy chief (if necessary) of the office. The two leaders also perform duties as lawyers, while directing the work of the office. As for the internal organizational set-up, there are no specific provisions in the Provisional Regulations Regarding Lawyers. Based on practical experience, the legal consultation offices of certain counties and cities consist of reception and litigation groups. The reception group is mainly responsible for receiving visitors, answering legal questions, and writing documents of complaint on others' behalf. The litigation group is responsible for acting as representatives in civil cases and for criminal defense. The two groups take turns to do the above-mentioned work. This practice enables every lawyer to have an opportunity to master different kinds of legal services and gives full rein to the capabilities of the individual lawyers and the collectives. This is a good form of organization.

Leadership and supervision Legal consultation offices are under the organizational leadership and supervision of state judicial administrative institutions. The practice of law, past and present in China, is different from that in the West. The non–governmental nature of legal practice in the West is inseparable from the Western legal tradition of retaining private lawyers for representation in legal cases, whereas China lacks this tradition. It will take a fairly long time before China produces lawyers who have a good mastery of professional legal knowledge and can provide the needed services for economic development, while following the socialist road. A great deal of difficult and complicated organizational work is needed to achieve this end. Therefore, at present, law offices are directed and supervised by state judicial administrative institutions.

The placement of law offices under the leadership and supervision of the state judicial administrative institutions facilitates the proper and rational development of lawyers and the legal profession. The judicial administrative institutions evaluate the qualifications of lawyers, mete out awards and penalties, administer ideological education, and provide professional training. They manage law offices by providing the operational expenses and assist lawyers organizations. This organizational structure of having the state judicial administrative institutions supervise and assist the law offices is suitable to the development of the attorney system and better provision of legal services in China.

Article 19 of the Provisional Regulations Regarding Lawyers provides that lawyers associations will be established in order to safeguard the legitimate rights and interests of lawyers, foster interchange, promote the development of legal services, and strengthen the ties of lawyers at home and abroad.

Lawyers associations have now been established in twenty-eight provinces, municipalities directly under Central Government and autonomous regions, except for Taiwan and Tibet. Under the guidance of the judicial administrative institutions and through their efforts, these associations have united and educated their members, and have actively carried out all

192

forms of service activities. According to incomplete statistics, they have, over the past few years, assisted judicial administrative institutions in holding over eighty meetings to exchange service experiences, published more than twenty kinds of magazines, and over four hundred editions of professional study materials and document compilations for lawyers. In short, they have done a great deal of valuable work in improving professional resources for lawyers, and in promoting the development of their services. They have also made great efforts in encouraging lawyers to perform their duties according to law, and in safeguarding the legitimate rights and interests of the legal profession. Meanwhile, they have worked to promote ties between lawyers in different parts of the country, and within the associations, and have carried out friendly exchanges with lawyers and legal associations of other countries.

With the founding of lawyers associations in all parts of China, the All-China Lawyers Association was established in July 1986. The Charter of the All-China Lawyers Association provides:

Organization The association is a popular social organization whose professional services are placed under the guidance of the Ministry of Justice. The aim of the association is to unite lawyers throughout the country, to constantly improve their organizational standing, to adhere to the four cardinal principles, to correctly put into practice Party and state principles, and policies concerning legal work, to serve the people whole-heartedly, while guaranteeing the correct application of the law so as to promote socialist democracy. The association also strives to improve the socialist legal system, and to advance China's socialist modernization.

Functions The functions of the All-China Lawyers Association are:

— To carry out, among its members, political and ideological education, and education in professional ethics, and to organize its members to study Party and state principles and policies, state laws and decrees, and relevant professional knowledge;

— To organize professional research activities of lawyers and to publish legal magazines and periodicals to improve the professional level of lawyers and promote the development of legal services;

—To support lawyers in the performance of their duties according to law, and to safeguard the legitimate rights and interests of its members;

—To provide professional information and reference materials to its members, as well as consultation services;

—To make proposals to relevant departments concerning the building of the legal system;

—To provide welfare services to its members;

—To coordinate the work of lawyers associations in the provinces, autonomous regions and municipalities directly under the Central Government; and

—To carry out exchanges with foreign lawyers and their organizations.

Membership All lawyers in China are members of the association and all the lawyers associations in the provinces, autonomous regions, and municipalities directly under the Central Government are group members of the association. The rights and obligations of the members are:

—To enjoy the right to elect and be elected cadres and of the association.

—To participate in research and related activities held by the association;

—To have access to books and reference materials of the association;

—To make suggestions to relevant departments on legal construction through the association;

—To make criticisms and suggestions on the work of the association;

—To supervise the financial expenditures of the association;

—To pay membership dues regularly; and

—To abide by the association's charter, implement its resolutions and complete the work entrusted by the association.

Sources of finance The sources of finance of the All-China Lawyers Association are state appropriations, financial revenues of the association, membership dues, and other legitimate revenues.

QUALIFICATIONS OF
CHINESE LAWYERS

Chinese lawyers are state legal workers. They are not professionals in the Western sense. They shoulder highly political and professional tasks and obligations. The Provisional Regulations Regarding Lawyers provide that the political requirements for lawyers are to love and support the People's Republic and the socialist system. These requirements are the same as those of the Constitution for citizens. In other words, politically, lawyers should be patriots first and foremost, and at the same time, they are revolutionaries who firmly adhere to the socialist road. By satisfying these two basic political requirements, lawyers working within socialist laws serve the fundamental interests of the state and the people by performing their services and guaranteeing the proper functioning of the socialist legal system. These are the fundamental differences between Chinese lawyers and lawyers of the Western countries.

Article 8 of the Provisional Regulations Regarding Lawyers delineates the political and professional requirements for Chinese lawyers. It stipulates that Chinese citizens who love and support the state and socialism, and who has the right to elect and be elected, upon passing a professional examination, may qualify as a lawyer, provided that one of the following conditions are met:

— College law graduates with two years of experience in judicial work, teaching, or legal research;

— Those who have received professional law training and have served as a judge on the people's court, or a procurator of the people's procuratorate;

— College graduates with three years of experience and legal and technical expertise in their field of economic, scientific or technological work, who have received additional professional legal training, and are suitable to serve as lawyers; and

— Those who have a college education or the equivalent, possess professional legal ability as listed in the first two items are suitable to serve as lawyers.

The above requirements are established only because of the present conditions in China. Because of the " cultural revolution" and other reasons, Chinese colleges turn out very few law graduates annually. It would be unrealistic for a while to make professional college degree legal training the prerequisite for legal practice. To meet the growing need for lawyers, all avenues for people of talent should be opened. Emphasis should be placed on combining professional knowledge and practical experience, and combining law college training with on the job training so more people can become lawyers to satisfy the increasing demands for legal services.

Articles 9 and 12 of the Provisional Regulations Regarding Lawyers provide for the qualification and disqualification of a lawyer. Article 9 stipulates that "Qualifications of an applicant shall be subject to examination and approval by judicial administrative departments of the provinces, autonomous regions, and municipalities directly under the Central Government. Those who meet qualification requirements shall be issued a license and reported to the Ministry of Justice for record. If the Ministry of Justice discovers any illegalities in the examination and approval, it shall notify the administrative department concerned to carry out a re-evaluation."

Examination and qualification of lawyers are very strict in China, as can be seen in Article 9. This approach guarantees both the political and practical proficiency of lawyers. Article 12 stipulates that "Lawyers who are incompetent shall be disqualified by the decision of the administrative departments of provinces, autonomous regions and municipalities directly under the Central Government, with approval of the Ministry of Justice." Strict qualification procedure prevents the lowering of standards whereby the number of lawyers increase but the level of competence decrease. This approach toward disqualification of lawyers is both necessary and prudent.

Article 10 of the Provisional Regulations Regarding Lawyers clearly stipulates that "Those who have acquired the qualification of a lawyer and cannot leave their posts may be part-time lawyers. They should be given support by their work units." According to China's attorney system, there are full-time and part-time lawyers. This is not only favorable for expanding the contingent of lawyers, but for relying on the people and putting the work of lawyers on the public basis. To en-

196

sure that a part-time lawyer can carry out his work as a lawyer more efficiently, his work unit should give him special considerations, provide him ample time and other favorable conditions so that he can work more efficiently in performing his duties as a lawyer. Article 10 also provides: "The working personnel of the people's courts, people's procuratorates and people's security institutions shall not work concurrently as lawyers." This provision seeks to prevent conflicts of interest and assures mutual cooperation and restraint between the lawyers on the one hand and the courts, security institutions and procuratorates on the other.

To increase the number of lawyers while maintaining the highest standards of proficiency, Article 11 of the Provisional Regulations Regarding Lawyers provides that " College law graduates and those who have received professional law training may become probational lawyers with the examination and approval of the judicial administrative departments of the provinces, autonomous regions and municipalities directly under the Central Government" and that "Their probational period is two years. After the two years, they will be qualified as lawyers according to provisions of Article 9. Those who fail to pass the examination may extend their period of probation." This provides a proper channel for training and selecting qualified persons as lawyers. After a period of practical work and after undergoing examination and evaluation, probational lawyers will become qualified lawyers, thus steadily expanding the contingent of lawyers, infusing the contingent with fresh blood, and meeting increasing needs for legal services.

To raise the professional efficiency of lawyers, the Ministry of Justice has established a three-tier training program of the central, provincial, and prefectural levels under unified leadership, with management at different levels. Lawyers are given general legal training and specialized training in economic laws and foreign economic laws so as to constantly improve their professional efficiency. Over the past few years, China has turned out quite a number of lawyers who are proficient in both law and economic affairs. In addition, the Ministry of Justice and many judicial administrative departments at the provincial, autonomous regional and municipal levels have actively assisted the state economic departments in holding different kinds of training courses on economic laws, and training legal advisors for enterprises. Over the past few years, they have trained a large number of legal personnel for enterprises, playing an active role in applying legal means in managing economic affairs.

GUIDING PRINCIPLE OF THE ACTIVITIES OF LAWYERS AND THEIR RIGHTS AND OBLIGATIONS

Article 3 of the Provisional Regulations Regarding Lawyers provides that "In carrying out their activities, lawyers shall take facts as the basis and law as the criterion." This is the basic principle guiding the activities of lawyers.

Taking facts as the basis requires that lawyers should never fail to distinguish between right and wrong, expose contradictions or clarify erroneous facts. They should not make irrational judgment in defending criminal cases as representatives in civil cases, or in carrying out other legal activities. In drafting complaints or other legal documents, they should reflect the objective truth, and the legitimate requirements of the parties instead of exaggerating or minimizing the facts, or concealing or distorting them.

Taking the law as the criterion requires lawyers, as defenders or representatives, to distinguish between right and wrong instead of making decisions at will. In answering legal questions or in offering legal advice, lawyers should strive to resolve disputes and prevent their recurrence while conscientiously protecting the legal rights and interests of the people.

The Provisional Regulations Regarding Lawyers provide for the following rights of lawyers:

—Lawyers enjoy protection by law in performing their duties according to law, and no interference from organizations and individuals is allowed.

—When participating in litigational activities, lawyers have the right to read materials in the record of the case and examine the evidence. They also have the right to see defendants in custody and communicate with them.

198

Lawyers have the right to make investigations and visits pertaining to the cases they handle.

—In public hearings, with the permission of the judge, the lawyers have the right to directly question defendants, witnesses, and expert witnesses, request the court to notify new witnesses to appear in court, obtain new evidence, or request re-examination or re-inspection of evidence;

—Lawyers have the right to refuse legal representation in a case if he feels that the defendant has failed to reveal the entire truth of the case.

—After the court pronounces judgment, with the consent of the defendant, lawyers have the right to appeal to a higher court.

Lawyers have the following obligations when performing their duties according to law:

— Lawyers must keep state secrets and maintain the confidentiality of private matters made known to them through their work.

—Lawyers should never collaborate with their client or client organization in fabricating or distorting facts, destroying evidence or resorting to deceptions of any kind.

— Lawyers should not accept private awards or appointments from clients.

CHAPTER *14*

People's Mediation System

For much of China's history, mediation has been used to settle disputes. Since antiquity, the common people have formed the habit of asking prestigious persons to mediate settlements in clans, villages or neighborhoods. As time passed, a fine tradition emerged. Since 1949, the Chinese Government has legally systematized this tradition of people's mediation. Everywhere, people's mediation committees have been established to facilitate the peaceful resolution of disputes.

People's mediation has now become an important part of China's socialist legal system. It has been praised by foreign friends as "an experience of the East." When a dispute arises, the contesting parties do not appear in court. They go to the local people's mediation committee, which is elected by local people, and is a self-managing organization. According to state laws and policies, as well as socialist morality and customs, the committee clarifies the facts of the dispute, judges between right and wrong, and exercises careful persuasion. It urges quarreling parties to treat each other in a spirit of mutual understanding and accommodation, so as to solve misunderstanding. Usually, the dispute is promptly resolved without hurting either party.

In 1954 the Chinese Government promulgated Provisional Regulations for Organizing People's Mediation Committees, which specify the nature, tasks, establishment, method, principles, and disciplines of the people's mediation committee. The regulations provide a legal foundation for mediation work.

Both the new Constitution and the Civil Procedure Law (tentative) enacted in 1982 fully affirm the important role played by the people's mediation system in China's political and social life. They clearly define the legal status of people's mediation in the state system. Stipulations concerning the people's mediation committees established in China's present Constitution and the Civil Procedure Law, as well as in the Provisional Regulations for Organizing People's Mediation Committees provide a foundation for understanding and studying China's people's mediation system.

DEVELOPMENT AND CHARACTERISTICS

Inheriting the fine tradition of past civilian mediation, the present people's mediation system in China has gradually developed and improved within the new historical circumstances of a half century of revolution and construction led by the Communist Party of China. Before 1949, some regulations for civilian mediation had been established in revolutionary base areas. For example, during the Anti-Japanese War and the People's War of Liberation, the Shaanxi-Gansu-Ningxia Border Area Government promulgated the Regulations for Mediating Civil and Criminal Cases in 1942. In 1947, the North China People's Government published the Decision on Mediating Civil Disputes.

After 1949, the Chinese Government attached importance to people's mediation and decided in 1953 to establish systematically and improve nationwide grassroots mass mediation. In March 1954, the government promulgated the Provisional Regulations for Organizing People's Mediation Committees. Those regulations specified the following principles:

—The mediation committee is a mass mediation organization working under the guidance of the people's government and people's court.

—The mediation committee's task is to mediate the settlement of common civil disputes and minor criminal cases and, through mediation, to publicize the legal system.

—Mediation committees are established in neighborhoods in cities and townships in the rural counties. A committee is composed of three to eleven persons.

—Members of the mediation committee are elected by representatives of residents of a neighborhood, or by a township people's congress under the administration of the people's government at the grassroots level. The committee is headed by a chairman and one or two deputy chairmen. They are elected by committee members and can serve consecutive terms. If a committee member violates the law, neglects duty, or is incompetent, he or she shall be replaced promptly by the original election organization.

— The mediation committee should take advantage of intervals between production work to listen to the disputing parties. It should carry out in-depth investigations. In mediating a settlement, committee members should arrive at their decisions after rational deliberation.

— If any mediation goes against state law or policy, the people's court should correct or annul it.

After the promulgation of the regulations, people's mediation developed rapidly throughout the country. According to the 1955 statistics, the mediation committees were established in seventy percent of China's townships and city neighborhoods. They helped settle large numbers of civil disputes.

After the Lin Biao and Jiang Qing counterrevolutionary cliques were defeated, especially after the Third Plenary Session of the Eleventh CPC Central Committee was held, the people's mediation system was fully affirmed by the Chinese Government as an important part of socialist democracy and legality. China re-established the Ministry of Justice and judicial institutions at all levels in 1979, which gave better guidance to people's mediation committees.

In 1980, the NPC Standing Committee republished the Provisional Regulations for Organizing People's Mediation Committees while the Ministry of Justice made a revision of the article on the establishment of the mediation committee. Since then the people's mediation system has developed and improved along with the mediation committees. By the end of 1985, the total number of mediation committees in China had grown to 930,000, with five million members. Mediation committees have also been established in factories and mines. They have been elected in ninety-seven percent of China's urban neighborhood committees, and township committees. From the beginning of

1981 to the middle of 1985, these mediation committees settled a total of approximately 32,510,000 civil disputes, and prevented 367,000 possible deaths.

In cooperation with related departments, people's mediation committees have launched drives for "Residents' pledges," "Five-good families" and "Clean and cultured courtyards, compounds and blocks." They have also helped remold juvenile delinquents.

This shows clearly that people's mediation is an essential part of China's legal system. Nevertheless, people's mediation is different from mediation conducted by the people's court or administrative institutions. According to law, China today has three kinds of mediation — court mediation, administrative mediation and people's mediation. Court mediation means that in the course of a lawsuit, the court persuades the disputing parties to settle their dispute in a spirit of mutual understanding and compromise. China's law considers this to be an important method for handling civil and criminal cases by the people's courts. Administrative mediation means that mediation is conducted under the leadership of related government administration with this duty. For example, Chapter 5 of the Economic Contract Law of the People's Republic of China specifies a method of mediating settlements of economic contract disputes between legal persons or between a legal person and an individual by industrial and commercial administrative institutions. People's mediation means that the people's mediation committee mediates between disputing civilians.

All three kinds of mediation have common characteristics. They are all aimed at solving disputes and improving the relations of disputing parties. All of them must conform to state laws and policies and use persuasion and education, while maintaining the principle of voluntary acceptance. They share the same purpose of increasing stability and unity, and promoting the four modernizations. Nevertheless, people's mediation is different from the others in principle. The differences are:

The different mediator The mediator of court mediation is the state judicial institution — the people's court. The mediator of administrative mediation is an administrative institution charged with the task of mediating settlements of disputes. The mediator of people's mediation is the people's mediation committee.

The different nature of mediation Court mediation takes place in the context of a lawsuit, a necessary legal procedure for the people's court to hear civil cases and prosecution of criminal cases. People's and administrative mediations, however, are outside of court action. They do not require initiation of a lawsuit, let alone a necessary legal proceeding.

The different object of mediation Court mediation can take place in any civil case or prosecution of a criminal case accepted by the court. The object of administrative mediation is generally limited to specific legal conflicts such as contract disputes. The object of people's mediation, however, is a "common" civil dispute — a domestic argument or a minor criminal affair. "Common" civil disputes involve unsophisticated matters where legitimate rights and interests are infringed upon, such as disputes over marriage, family affairs, the support of aged parents, the bringing up of children, inheritances, debts, housing, estates, land, forests, water conservancy facilities, livestock, farm implements, the destruction of property, and other matters in life and production. Disputes over minor criminal cases involve light injuries, interfering in the freedom of marriage, damaging one's reputation, persecuting family members, abandoning one's wife, and so on.

The different effect of mediation When an agreement on court mediation is reached, it takes the same effect as a verdict, with the binding force of compulsory law. Both parties must abide by the agreement. If one party fails to do so, the other party has the right to appeal to the people's court for enforcement. An understanding or agreement reached under the people's mediation committee is chiefly bound by the promises and mutual trust of the disputing parties, and by the force of public opinion and morality. Both parties fulfill the agreement voluntarily without the coercion of law. If one party backs out of its bargain, or both parties do so, they have the right to appeal to court, and no person or organization can stop or interfere with them. This is similar to administrative mediation.

ROLE OF PEOPLE'S MEDIATION

People's mediation plays a vital part in the building of China's socialist legal system. Its role embodies the following aspects.

Increasing unity among the people and establishing a new socialist relationship between individual Chinese It is impossible for people in society to avoid disputes. Civil controversies involve not only the personal interests of quarreling parties, but also relatives, friends, and work units. If they are not promptly settled, disputes will affect the unity of the people. Those on the people's mediation committee come from the masses and live among them. They are familiar with the people, the environment and surrounding conditions. They can detect quickly civil disputes and mediate settlements without exacerbating the already ruffled feelings of each party. They help improve relations and promote unity. According to statistics, people's mediation committees in all parts of China in 1982 settled a total of eight million disputes, and eradicated conflicts and misunderstanding among tens of millions of persons.

For example, there was a farmer, Ma, living in Dashita Village in Xingcheng County, Liaoning Province. A dispute flared up between him and his wife. The wife left home and traveled a great distance to her mother's and did not return for a long time. She appealed to a court for divorce. The village mediation committee investigated the case. It held that Ma and his wife had been on good terms before and after their wedding, and their marriage had not yet been broken irreparably. It was possible to patch up their differences. The mediation committee sent three persons to the home of the wife's mother. They had heart-to-heart talks with the wife and her parents for three days and evenings. They persuaded the wife to restore good relations with her husband. This divorce dispute was solved before the court took up the matter.

Preventing civil disputes from becoming acute and endangering life and property, reducing unlawful acts and criminal cases, and strengthening public order The majority of civil disputes appear to be trifling. If they are not promptly handled or properly settled, they may develop into criminal cases or cases

205

which disturb public order, such as homicide, suicide, arson, and assault. Public order and social stability are at stake. Therefore, people's mediation can resolve civil disputes as soon as they arise and prevent them from worsening. According to 1982 statistics, China's people's mediation committees succeeded through timely intervention in saving a total of 105,000 persons from suicide, homicide and deadly injuries.

In Changde Prefecture, Hunan Province, the great majority of people's mediation committees accept and hear disputes as soon as they are submitted and do not wait until the next day. All common disputes are settled in villages without going to court. Since the beginning of 1982, people's mediation in the prefecture has accommodated numerous disputes that would have caused two thousand suicides, one thousand homicides, and two thousand armed assaults.

Living in Shimen County in that prefecture, a farm contractor named Wang once sold a truck to a Wu. Wu got the truck and failed to pay for it over a period of time. The two men quarreled. Wu drove the truck away. Taking some explosives and detonators, Wang went to look for Wu. He planned to blow up both Wu and the truck.

Receiving word of the incident, the local people's mediation committee sent persons to search for Wang, and brought him home in five days. Through mediation and persuasion, the committee settled the dispute, defended Wang's legitimate rights and interests, and prevented an aggravated case. This case demonstrates that people's mediation is essential for the maintenance of public order.

Reducing people's lawsuits and relieving the burden of the people's court so that it can focus its attention on major civil and criminal cases According to statistics in 1981 and 1982, the total number of civil disputes solved by mediation committees in China is more than ten times the total number of civil cases accepted by grassroots courts.

Heightening morality and a sense of law of the public One of the regular tasks of the people's mediation committee is to publicize laws and promote moral education among the people. While intervening in disputes, the people's mediation committee adopts various methods and uses lucid and understandable language to explain the socialist legal system to the public to foster a new morality and custom. The committee members tell the public what is meant by legal and illegal, what their rights and duties are, what they should support and what they should oppose. This improves knowledge of the laws in the public, and increases their sense of observing law, removes feudal ideas and customs, and cultivates a socialist morality.

Promoting the four modernizations A. As the people's mediation committees settle large numbers of civil disputes, people are freed from stress so that they can have peace of mind to concentrate their energies on work. **B.** Since the people's mediation committee is established at the grassroots level, it is close to people and easily accessible to any dispute. Mediation is convenient to the people and helps them avoid delay in work and production. **C.** Generally speaking, civil disputes hold up production to some extent, especially farmers' disputes over crop-lands, water, livestock, and farm implements and machinery. Speedily solving such disputes, the people's mediation committee helps maintain economic order and directly promotes production. **D.** Resolving disputes among the people, the people's mediation committee helps leaders of grassroots departments and production units disentangle themselves from small disputes and focus their attention on giving guidance to production and other work. This ensures the success of various kinds of grassroots work. **E.** As the people's mediation committees settle large numbers of civil disputes, improve the social fabric of life and keep public order, they help various areas and units maintain normal order of production, work, and life. This facilitates the stability and unity of society as a whole, and creates a good social environment for achieving the four modernizations.

All these activities indicate that people's mediation means much to the development of socialist democracy and the building of a legal system with Chinese characteristics. The people's mediation committee is a Chinese invention. It embodies the stipulation of the Constitution that all state power belongs to the people, who manage social affairs by various means and forms according to law. The development of people's mediation is an important means of strengthening and expanding people's democratic rights. Besides, people's mediation is a good form of integrating China's judicial institutions with people's self–managing organizations. It is a key measure adopted by judicial institutions to rely on the masses. China has a large population and a vast territory where the development of economy and culture in various areas is not well-balanced. Dependence on judicial institutions alone is not enough to perfect the legal system and govern the country according to law. Practice has shown that people's mediation is a powerful ally of the people's governments and judicial institutions at various levels in handling civil disputes. It is basic to judicial work and enjoys great popularity. It is a reliable guarantee for perfecting the legal system. We expect China's people's mediation system will develop further, improve and contribute to strengthening socialist democracy and legality, and to building socialist material and spiritual civilization.

PRINCIPLES AND PROCEDURE

According to the Constitution, the Civil Procedure Law (tentative), and Provisional Regulations for Organizing People's Mediation Committees, the people's mediation committees established in China's cities and villages are people's self-managing organizations. Their purpose is to mediate civil disputes by persuasion and education, so as to prevent such disputes from becoming acute. Mediation unites the people, maintains social stability, enhances the public sense of law and morality, and promotes the building of a socialist civilization. To achieve this goal, people's mediation committees and their staff must follow these work principles:

Conducting mediation according to state laws and policies The resolution of civil disputes must be based on laws and policies, rather than the demands of any party, feudal customs, or old social mores. Similarly, right and wrong must be distinguished by legal criteria rather than by subjective impressions. By relying on laws and policies, mediators can help each party assume responsibility so impasses in their dispute can be resolved. A reconciliation can be reached only when the disputing parties can distinguish right from wrong. Mediation protects the legitimate rights and interests of the parties while allowing the party in error to learn from the experience. This process helps eliminate wrongful influences in society and fosters a better mode of life.

People's mediation committees and their mediators must adhere strictly to laws. If the law has no applicable provisions pertaining to the dispute at hand, mediators must refer to state policies. If neither laws nor state policies are applicable, mediators should rely on socialist moral standards and seek truth from facts.

When a people's mediation committee is confronted by difficult problems it can go to the grassroots government or court for instructions. If the mediators violate laws and policies and arrive at an unwise agreement, the grassroots government or court has the right to correct or void the agreement according to the Provisional Regulations for Organizing People's Mediation Committees.

Having the consent of both disputing parties and refraining from coercing a settlement The people's mediation committee must pay attention to the will of both parties and use patient persuasion. It must not apply force, pressure, or threat. Both parties must reach an agreement and execute the agreement on a voluntary basis. They must not accept it reluctantly. If they cannot arrive at an agreement, they must not be coerced.

Mediation is not a necessary alternative to litigation No one shall stop a disputing party from bringing the dispute before the court because it has not gone through mediation, or because the mediation has failed. People's mediation plays an important part in promptly settling civil disputes, strengthening unity and stability, and reducing the number of lawsuits. But, by no means does this signify that all disputes must go through mediation before going to court. Every citizen in China has the right to bring a case before the court to defend one's legitimate rights and interests. This right is written in the Constitution. No person, organization, or institution shall infringe upon this right. Nor shall the people's mediation committee do so. People's mediation is a non-legal action, not a necessary procedure of law. Therefore, the people's mediation committee must respect the people's right to litigation as a fundamental principle.

The general procedure for people's mediation follows:

Accepting disputes There are two ways of accepting disputes. One way is that one or both of the disputing parties goes to the people's mediation committee to ask for intervention. The other way is for the mediation committee to detect the dispute and offer mediation.

Investigation and analysis The mediation committee conducts an investigation to clarify the nature, cause, process, and focus of a dispute, and found out the influential people behind it. It then makes a comprehensive analysis of the dispute, and judges between right and wrong.

Mediating between disputing parties through persuasion The mediation committee must mediate on the basis of facts obtained from investigation. It must refer to state laws, policies, and socialist morality as criteria, and refrain from unprincipled compromises. It should conduct private mediation of simple disputes involving secrets of the disputing parties, or disputes not fit for making public. For complicated disputes involving a large circle of persons and serious consequence, the people's mediation committee may ask representatives of the people, leaders of the units where the disputing parties work, and their relatives and friends, to join in the mediation.

Urging the disputing parties to reconcile their dispute and come to an agreement When persuasion has helped the disputing parties reach a common understanding and has provided an ideological basis for an agreement, the mediators should seize the opportunity to encourage the parties to bring about a reconciliation of their own accord. The disputing parties should make self-criticisms and apologies, guarantee the rectification of past errors, return things, or compensate for losses. If they fail to achieve a consensus, the mediation committee should propose a reasonable solution and persuade them to seek common ground on major issues while reserving differences on minor ones. It should urge them to consult fully with each other, accept a correct solution and arrive at an agreement.

Executing the agreement An agreement negotiated through people's mediation is different from a court decision or ruling, or from one concluded through court mediation. Having no legal compulsory force, it depends on the promises and mutual trust of the disputing parties, as well as the force of public opinion and morality for execution. The agreement is executed on a moral duty, not a legal one.

A Shanghai people's mediation committee's mediation of the settlement of a divorce dispute in the presence of a judicial delegation from the Federal Republic of Germany in 1984 helps clarify the principles and procedure of people's mediation.

On the afternoon of December 3, 1984 the judicial delegation from West Germany paid a visit to Wusong Road in Shanghai to watch how the mediation committee of the Nantang Neighborhood Residents Committee mediated between a Zhou and his wife Shen. Family chores led to a dispute between husband and wife after their marriage. Carrying their baby son with her, the wife went to live with her parents and did not return home. Later the parents of both husband and wife blamed each other, and the dispute developed into a fight between the two families, all of which left the wife and husband in despair. The wife appealed to the court for divorce. At this juncture, the people's mediation committee intervened with the cooperation of the units where the two worked. It also talked repeatedly to the parents. The committee finally succeeded in helping the couple overcome practical difficulties. The committee's painstaking work caused the wife to withdraw her appeal for divorce and return home to live with her husband. The mediation committee called a reconciliation meeting, where the two parties made self-criticisms, and removed all misunderstandings in their minds. The husband and wife agreed to allow China's German friends attend the meeting.

The head of the Nantang People's Mediation Committee presided over the gathering, which was attended by members of the committee, the disputing parties, and representatives of their work units, totaling eight persons. With encouragement from the mediators, both disputing parties gave self-criticisms according to related articles of the Marriage Law. They finally signed an agreement ensuring that husband and wife would live together harmoniously by respecting and loving each other, and sharing joint responsibility for family chores.

At the end of the one hour and twenty minute meeting, the

head of the delegation Staatssekretar Benno Erhard delivered a warm speech saying,

Members of my delegation and I think your mediation committee has played a very important part in settling the dispute between the husband and wife. We greatly admire your retired personnel [the mediators] for dedicating themselves to this significant purpose. We are very pleased. We are going to take your experience home. Of course, the circumstances of the legal system here are very different from ours. But we want to see how your legal system works. Today we got an answer. For this, we express our heartfelt thanks. Before leaving here, I wish you would reunite more and more disputing families. The practice of our Federal Republic of Germany has shown that if there is widespread familial disharmony, the whole society suffers as if from a malignant disease. I gained a good deal of enlightenment from observing your mediation today. In the course of your mediation, I have observed, the minds of the disputing parties undergoing changes. This lady's thoughts, in particular, have taken a radical transformation. Such changes in our country would play an important part in building more happy homes. As we march ahead toward a new era, both peoples must guard against allowing minor issues to obstruct real social progress.

CHAPTER *15*

Status Que and Prospects for China's Legal System

Since October 1949, especially since the historical meeting in 1978, China has moved deliberately, though not without setbacks, toward the development of its legal system. This process has been in keeping with the CPC Central Committee's policy of building and improving the socialist legal system. The Constitution and a series of laws and regulations have been issued or revised, marking a new stage in the country's legal development.

These laws have had a great effect on the nation's social, political, and economic life. Through harsh penalties against criminal offenses and economic crimes, and through educating and reforming criminals as part of a comprehensive approach to maintaining law and order, the entire nation's legal consciousness has been raised, and social stability guaranteed. The current policy to publicize legal knowledge throughout the country has strengthened China's socialist democracy and legal system. The country is creating a sound legal environment, where laws provide rules for citizens to follow and are strictly enforced.

From January 1979 to August 1986, China saw the birth of a new Constitution and many laws and regulations. The NPC and its Standing Committee promulgated fifty-two laws, nineteen amendments, and twenty-nine resolutions concerning legal issues, and endorsed seven regulations and resolutions. In the same period, the State Council issued over four hundred administrative decrees, and the people's congresses and their standing committees in the provinces, autonomous regions, and municipalities directly under the Central Government passed 749 local regulations. These laws and regulations serve as an essential basis for a Chinese-style socialist legal system.

At the moment, a large number of laws concerning economic, cultural and educational fields are in the making. These include laws on copyright, intellectual property, state-owned enterprises, companies, bankruptcy, lawyers, educational funds, and teachers. The birth of a complete legal procedure is fundamental to ensuring the democratic, scientific and authoritative features of the Chinese legal system. It has also established a basis for the application of law throughout the country.

CONSTITUTION AND STATE LAWS

The Constitution is the fundamental law of China shaping the form of all other laws. It is the essential component in China's legal machine. Nothing in other laws and regulations should contradict its principles. State laws concern the creation of state institutions, their functions and mutual relations, and are also known as constitutional laws. As the crystallization of constitutional provisions on the state system, they include the Organic Law of the People's Courts (passed in 1954, revised in July 1979 and September 1983), the Organic Law of Local People's Congresses and Local Governments at Various Levels (passed in September 1954, revised in July 1979, December 1982, and 1986), the Organic Law of the State Council (passed in December 1982), the Organic Law of the National People's Congress (passed in September 1954, revised in December 1982), and the Law on Regional National Autonomy (passed in May 1984). The Constitution and these state laws have drawn a clear picture for the state system.

The Constitution and state laws are closely related, so each amendment in the former brings about revisions in the latter. The Constitution now in effect was promulgated in 1982 and preceded by those in 1954, 1975, and 1978. Therefore, all state laws were made or revised after 1982. In conjunction with the Constitution, they have defined China's state system, the major tasks of the state, and the basic principles governing the activities of the state apparatus:

1. The People's Republic of China is a socialist country under the people's democratic dictatorship and led by the proletariat on the basis of a worker-peasant alliance. Socialism is the political system of the country where all power belongs to the people. The people exercise state power through the NPC and local people's congresses, and run state, social, economic and cultural affairs through the means and channels provided by the laws.

The people in China enjoy sufficient democracy. All delegates to the NPC and local people's congresses at various levels are elected by, responsible to, and supervised by the people.

The Election Law outlines the election system and procedure. The current election system features:

—Direct election being expanded from the grassroots to the county level;

—A tiered election;

—The secret ballot;

—A divided constituency according to either working units or residential areas;

— Provisions on nomination procedure and preliminary elections; and

—Provisions on election recall procedure.

The state apparatus runs under the principle of democratic centralism. The institutions of state power — the administration, the judiciary, the procuratorate, and the military — work in cooperation, each exercising its functions and power independently. Within the judiciary system, procuratorate authorities, the court and procuratorate restrict as well as cooperate with each other.

In regard to the division of legislative power, the central state apparatus maintains complete, but flexible, reign. It does, however, give full play to the initiative of the local state apparatus.

All national groups within the People's Republic of China are equal. The state safeguards the rights and lawful interests of national minorities, and defends and promotes equality, solidarity and mutual assistance among the nationalities. The state also stimulates economic and cultural development in areas inhabited by national minorities. In their own areas, which are inseparable parts of the People's Republic, the minority nationalities exercise autonomy.

2. The fundamental task of state laws is to guarantee the socialist modernization drive. After the eradication of the exploiting classes, the major contradiction in society lies in the backwardness of the productive forces on one hand and the need to improve the material and cultural aspects of the people's lives on the other. The Chinese people recognize the urgent need to improve the latter by concentrated development of the productive forces in society. This recognition is based on the four decades of experiences since the founding of the People's Republic. The latest 1982 Constitution contains the following statement in its preface: "The fundamental task of the state henceforth is to fulfill the socialist modernization." With the construction of socialist modernization put into the Constitution as the common goal of the whole nation, the development of China's legal system is set in the right direction.

As for the state economic system, the Constitution states clearly that socialist public ownership, namely, national ownership and collective ownership of the means of production, is the basis of China's economic system. However, private enterprise, as an important complement to the public sector, is also protected by the state.

The state protects public properties and forbids all organizations and individuals to seize or damage state-owned and collectively-owned properties through any means. The state also protects the lawful private incomes of citizens such as bank savings, housing and other properties, and the right to inherit private properties as well.

To accelerate the development of the national economy, China allows foreign economic entities and individuals to invest in the country according to its laws. They may practice various forms of economic cooperation with Chinese firms and other economic organizations. Cooperative takes place with joint ventures, joint operations, and independent foreign ventures. Economic cooperation has set specific goals and tasks for economic legislation, especially legislation on business contacts with foreign enterprises and individuals.

3. The state should safeguard the unity and dignity of the socialist legal system, and keep the system authoritative and strict. Socialist democracy must be developed, and the unity and dignity of the legal system must be maintained if the Chinese people are to exercise their power as masters of the state. Learning from the painful lessons of the "cultural revolution," China now attaches great importance to upholding the unity and dignity of the legal system. The Chinese Government has incorporated clear provisions demanding that all state departments, military forces, political parties, social organizations, businesses and institutions abide by the Constitution and laws. No political parties, organizations or individuals have the privilege to go beyond these strictures, and all violations must be investigated.

China stresses the unity and dignity of its legal system not only in terms of law enforcement and education, but also through legislation. Primary legal prominence is given to the Constitution. No law or administrative decree, central or local, should contain any materials or references contradictory to the Constitution. The Constitution provides that the NPC, as the highest source of state power, and its Standing Committee, have the power to supervise laws, rescind administrative decrees, decisions, and orders made by the State Council in contradiction to the Constitution and laws, and abolish local regulations and resolutions that run counter to the Constitution, laws and national decrees. Thus the legal system is guaranteed by legislation and judicature, greatly increasing its unity and dignity.

CRIMINAL LAWS

China has established a complete criminal justice system to defend the democratic dictatorship, national and collective properties, lawful private properties, and the personal, democratic and other rights of the citizen. This promotes social order, and ensures the success of the socialist revolution and construction.

In the early years of the People's Republic, a number of criminal regulations were enacted, such as Prohibitions on the

217

Export and Import of State Currency, Tentative Penalties for Impairing the State Currency, Tentative Regulations on Keeping State Secrets, Penalties Against Counterrevolutionaries in the People's Republic of China (passed in February 1951), Penalties on Corruption in the People's Republic of China, Tentative Ways of Controlling Counterrevolutionaries (promulgated in April 1952), Bans on Opium, and Tentative Bans on the Export of Valuable Cultural Relics and Books (passed in August 1956).

In July 1979, the Criminal Law of the People's Republic of China and the Criminal Procedure Law of the People's Republic of China were passed at the Second Session of the Fifth NPC and issued through decrees by the chairman of the Standing Committee.

After these laws were promulgated on January 1, 1980, the NPC Standing Committee passed a resolution to punish criminals who escape from jail or who commit new crimes after their release from reform through labor. It also passed resolutions on the review of capital punishment cases and on the time limitation for criminal cases. In March 1982, the NPC Standing Committee decided to impose severe punishment on criminals convicted of notorious economic crimes. In September 1983, the NPC Standing Committee decided to use speedy procedure to adjudicate criminals who caused serious breaches of public order and increased the severity of their punishment. In 1984, the NPC Standing Committee amended the time limitation for criminal cases. These efforts helped complete China's criminal legislation and brought China closer to a Chinese-style criminal justice system.

The Criminal Law of the People's Republic of China, revised and improved after 38 drafts, falls into two parts, 13 chapters and 192 articles. Part One contains general provisions concerning crimes and penalties. It consists of 89 articles in five chapters: guidelines, tasks, and range of effect of the Criminal Law; crimes; penalties; the application of penalties; and other provisions.

Part Two specifies crimes and corresponding penalties. It contains 103 articles in eight chapters: counterrevolutionary crime; jeopardizing public security; breaking socialist economic order; infringing on citizens' personal and democratic rights; trespassing on property; obstructing social administrative order; wrongfully interfering with marriage and family life; and dereliction of duty.

The Criminal Law has the following features:

—It distinguishes clearly between criminal and non—criminal offenses. It does not define minor offenses such as pilfering, small—scale gambling, and other kinds of misbehavior in the same category. Conducts which gravely jeopardize society for which administrative or disciplinary punishments are not enough are defined as crimes. Generally, these offenses are given lighter punishments than those given to counterrevolutionary crimes and grave criminal offenses. The law allows probation for some cases. Some light offenses can even be exempted from criminal punishments. Only offenses committed through vile means and with grave results are punished severely.

The principle of equality before the law applies to all crimes and to all criminals. Judges are banned from arbitrary judgments, cruel judgments, and judgments influenced by the social positions of the parties. All unwarranted arrest, search and interrogation, as well as interrogation by torture, are illegal. These provisions in the Criminal Law are conducive to protecting the innocent and punishing the guilty.

—The Criminal Law reflects the policy of combining punishment with leniency, imposing varying penalties on criminals depending on their offenses. For example, minors, accomplices, and criminals who have voluntarily surrendered themselves or supplied evidence, get lighter punishments than the recidivists, on habitual offenders in a case.

The Criminal Law stipulates that "Capital punishment is applied only to criminals who are convicted of the most heinous offenses." Some heinous criminals are sentenced to death with two years stay of the execution of sentence with a chance to reform themselves through labor. Most criminals who are not sentenced to death undergo the reform through labor program, a major type of sentence. Legal punishments fall into two categories: primary and secondary punishments. The latter include fines, deprivation of political rights and confiscation of property. They may supplement the primary ones such as public surveillance, labor in custody, definite imprisonment, life imprisonment and death. Foreign offenders may be expelled from China as a punishment, or as a complement to other punishments. All the punishments except death are aimed at reforming criminals. The law also allows release on parole and mitigation of sentence.

— The Criminal Law is a combination of principles and flexible approaches. It clearly defines crime, categories of crime, degrees of severity of various crimes, types of penalties, their application, and the range of penalties for various crimes. For example, Article 79 states clearly that "Offenses not included in the detailed definitions may be judged and sentenced by reference to articles on similar crimes, but the case should be submitted to the Supreme People's Court for examination." In the range of penalties for particular crimes, flexible or complementary regulations may be made for autonomous regions by the state institutions at the provincial level according to the political, economic and cultural features of the local nationalities. These adjustments must be in line with the general principles of the Criminal Law. The regulations are subjected to ratification by the NPC Standing Committee.

The Criminal Procedure Law of the People's Republic of China falls into four parts, 17 chapters and 164 articles. Part One covers general provisions, stating the guidelines, function and basic rules of the procedure law. It makes provisions on jurisdiction, recusal, argument, evidence, coercive measures, supplementary civil actions, time period and service. Part Two covers the registration, investigation, and public prosecution of a case, restrictions on investigation, and matters concerning public prosecution. Part Three pertains to the trial process. It elaborates on tribunals, trial procedure, procedure for review of death sentences, and trial supervision procedure. Part Four concerns the execution of sentences, including sentencing authorities, places and other issues involved in the execution of sentence.

The Criminal Procedure Law defines the principles, procedure and inter-relations for the court, the procuratorate and public security authorities in handling criminal cases. It outlines an evidentiary system and the rights and obligations of all people involved in lawsuits. It is a complete and scientific criminal procedure law.

The law establishes principal rules of criminal procedure for the law-enforcing bodies to follow in handling lawsuits. This enables the public to supervise the handling of the suits. The principles are:

— Only the court, procuratorate, and public security authorities have judicial power. No other organization and individuals are allowed to encroach on their power or hamper their operations;

— Law-enforcement bodies should rely on the masses in their operations;

— Evidence and the law are the only criteria for handling cases;

— All citizens are equal before the law;

— The court exercises jurisdiction, the procuratorate handles public prosecution, and the public security institutions investigate on the basis of cooperation and mutual restraint;

— All lawsuits are adjudicated in local languages;

— All cases are tried publicly except for those concerning state secrets, highly personal matters, and minor criminals. The judgments of closed court trials are also made public;

— The accused has the right to defense, and the exercise of this right is protected by court;

— A jury system is in effect. Except for minor criminal cases and suits brought by individuals, all first trials are handled by a bench of judges or a bench combined of judges and jurors; and

— The rights of all participants in a lawsuit are protected by the law.

The Criminal Procedure Law sets up an evidentiary system for criminal proceedings. Evidence, which means all facts collected by judiciary departments through lawful channels, is admissible. Criminal evidence falls into six categories: material and documentary evidence; testimony; testimony of a victim; statements and exculpations of defendants; conclusions of expert evaluations; and notes of on the spot search and examinations. Verdicts must be based on truthful evidence, and torture is prohibited as means of obtaining evidence. A defendant is not declared guilty if no evidence is available except his own confession, but he can be found guilty without his own confes-

221

sion when evidence is sufficient to prove him guilty.

The Criminal Procedure Law stipulates criminal procedure and compulsory measures in criminal proceedings. The law allows judicial institutions and personnel to release suspects on bail while awaiting trial. Judicial institutions and personnel may legally take coercive measures against defendants, to wit, house arrest, detention and arrest. Arrests are made to prevent suspects from evading prosecution, destroying evidence, and committing murder or suicide. The law, however, prohibits judicial institutions and personnel from making illegal arrests and detentions or invading the personal rights of citizens.

The Criminal Procedure Law stipulates the procedure for filing a case, investigation, initiation of public prosecution, first trial, second trial, and the procedure for death sentence review, supervision of trials, and execution of sentences. China's criminal procedure also features the following points:

—All parties in a suit have the right to appeal to a higher court against the verdict of the court of first instance, while the procuratorate concerned in the first trial has the right to make a counter-appeal. The appeal itself does not add to the sentence of the accused. Second trials are final, against which no appeals or counter-appeals shall be made;

—Death sentences are subject to review by higher courts to avoid mistakes; and

—All parties concerned in a case, and any other citizens may appeal to the court against a verdict already made. A people's court and procuratorate at a higher level have the right to call a re-trial if they find errors in the original verdict.

CIVIL LAWS

Civil legislation, covering every area of the people's social and personal life, is an important part of China's legal system. To protect the civil rights and lawful interests of the state, collectives, individuals and legal persons, the Chinese legislature has always kept as its goal the establishment of a complete and impartial civil law system.

As far back as 1950, China promulgated the Tentative Procedure for Government Departments, State Business and Cooperatives for the Making of Contracts, the Marriage Law of the People's Republic of China, and other special laws and regulations, and was preparing for a civil statute book and a civil procedure law. By 1982, the Civil Procedure Law of the People's Republic of China (for trial implementation) was issued, and the fourth draft of a civil statute book had been worked out. But China had just started a reform of the national economic system, and the situation was not yet proper for issuing a civil statute book. So, China made special laws from each of the more urgent areas.

In the past few years, the NPC Standing Committee issued a number of special civil laws such as the Economic Contract Law of the People's Republic of China (passed in December 1981), the Law of the People's Republic of China on Economic Contracts Involving Foreign Parties (passed in March 1985), the Patent Law of the People's Republic of China (passed in March 1984), the Trademark Law of the People's Republic of China (passed in August 1982), the Marriage Law of the People's Republic of China (passed in 1950 and revised in September 1980), and the Inheritance Law of the People's Republic of China (passed in April 1985). These laws have played a significant role in settling civil disputes.

On the other hand, common issues such as the legal status of citizens and legal persons, civil practice, civil agency, civil rights, civil responsibilities still lack specific provisions. Moreover, civil disputes, especially economic disputes, have increased tremendously in the last few years and require a comprehensive code for regulating civil activities and settling civil disputes.

A code of general civil rules pertaining to common issues in civil law could now be issued. Recent experiences from drafting special legislation and reforming the economic system, including opening to the outside world and handling economic and civil disputes, in addition to traditional approaches, the issuance of the Civil Procedure Law of the People's Republic of China, and the fourth draft of a civil dispute resolution, had made this possible. In April 1986, the first General Rules of Civil Law of the People's Republic of China was published. Although it excludes thorny problems, it is more flexible than a civil statute book and

223

is the nearest thing to the completion of civil legislation.

The General Rules of Civil Law, passed in 1986 at the Fourth Session of the Sixth NPC, took effect on January 1, 1987. The 156 articles of the general rules fall into nine chapters as general provisions, the citizen, the legal person, civil legal activities and agency, civil rights, civil responsibilities, limitation of proceedings, application of the rules on civil disputes involving foreign parties, and supplementary provisions. We see here the cornerstone of the Chinese civil judicial system.

The general rules present the basic principles in civil activities and their effect. The basic principles are:

—All participants in a civil proceeding are equal;

—Civil activities should be based on willingness, fairness, honesty and making an exchange at equal value;

—Civil rights and lawful interests of citizens and legal persons are protected by the law;

—Civil activities must be kept within the limits of the law and state policies;

—Civil activities are not allowed to trample on social justice or harm public interests, state economic plans, and social economic order; and

—Civil activities in the People's Republic of China fall under the power of the law.

The general rules stipulate clearly that the Civil Law of the People's Republic of China regulates property and personal relationships among citizens, among legal persons, and between citizens and legal persons. First of all, it regulates property relationship in two areas: A. In civil law, regulations of the property relationships is, in fact, a reflection of commodity exchange relationships when the status and rights of all parties are equal; B. Civil law mainly regulates property relationships between equal subjects, while the vertical relationship between the state and enterprises, or between enterprises and their branches or sections, is subject to economic laws and administrative regulations.

Civil law also regulates personal relationships in society. Civil and criminal laws protect these rights of an individual: the right to have one's good name protected, the right to keep one's image free from infringement or unauthorized use, and the right to a healthy life. Protection under the laws are also given to legal persons. They have the concurrent right to have their good names and titles protected.

The general rules are the foundation of civil rights in China. All citizens and legal persons may engage in civil activities, shoulder civil responsibilities, and are protected by civil rights.

Every citizen is entitled to civil rights from birth. A citizen's civil legal capacity is divided into three categories. Persons over eighteen years old, and persons from sixteen to eighteen years old who are self-sufficient, have full legal capacity. Minors over ten years old and mentally ill persons with the ability to be responsible for some of their actions enjoy limited legal capacity. The latter may engage in civil activities suitable to their age, intelligence and mental state, provided that they acted with permission from their guardians, or that such actions were taken by their guardians or legal agent on their behalf. Children under ten years old and mentally ill persons who are not accountable for their actions do not have legal capacity. Those in this category must act in civil matters through their legal guardians or agents.

Organizations considered legal persons under the law have civil rights and legal capacity. They also have civil responsibilities. To be considered a legal person, an organization must meet the following requirements: establishment by legal procedure; possession of the necessary assets or funds; possession of its own organization, title and place; and independent assumption of civil responsibilities.

Legal persons can be classified as business corporations, institutional entities and social organizational entities. The civil rights and legal capacity of a legal person begin with its legal incorporation and ends with its dissolution.

Civil legislation allows private cooperatives, self-employed industrial or commercial businesses, and rural families operating under contracts, to engage in civil activities. The law protects their civil rights and interests, and encourages them to cooperate with state businesses and institutions in economic activities.

The general rules establish other systems within the scope of civil law. These systems include the civil legal activity, proxy, civil rights, civil responsibility, and limitation of action. China has promulgated special laws and regulations governing marriage, inheritance, contracts, patent and trademark systems.

The Civil Procedure Law of the People's Republic of China was passed and issued at the Twenty-Second Session of the Fifth NPC Standing Committee in March 1982. It took effect on October 1 the same year. It is divided into five parts, 23 chapters and 205 articles. Part One consists of general provisions defining the tasks and fundamental principles of the Civil Procedure Law, jurisdiction, tribunals, recusal, parties in litigation, evidence, limitation of action, service, coercive measures against those obstructing civil proceedings, and court costs. Part Two covers first trial procedure, which includes an ordinary procedure, a simple procedure, and a special procedure. Part Three covers second trial procedure and the trial-supervising procedure. Part Four contains provisions on transfer, application, measures, suspension, and ordinary issues in implementation of civil procedure. The last part comprises special provisions on the general principles, arbitration, service, limitation of action, and judicial assistance of suits involving foreign parties.

The Civil Procedure Law and the General Rules of Civil Law form the first systematic civil legislation since the founding of the People's Republic and marks a significant step forward in China's civil legislation.

ECONOMIC LEGISLATION

Economic legislation refers to the economic laws and regulations that enable the state to organize, regulate and manage the economy directly through legal means. Economic legislation started with the development of overall economic reforms throughout the country and under new conditions of revitalizing the national economy and opening to the outside world. Before economic legislation was passed, many economic regulations were issued in the forms of government directions and decrees. In urgent circumstances during that period, the decrees played an important role in the restoration and development of production. However, they cannot work alone in the context of rapid development of modern economic construction now. What is needed is an organic combination of economic, legal and administrative means that rely more on economic laws in managing the economy. Therefore, it has become an urgent task for the Chinese legislature to legalize and regularize major and effective economic measures, thus making them relatively stable and authoritative for a period of time.

In the past, China issued over nineteen hundred important laws and regulations, of which seventy percent were economic ones. China's economic legislation did not begin seriously until 1979. Deng Xiaoping emphasized,

> So we must concentrate on enacting criminal and civil codes, procedural laws and other necessary laws concerning factories, people's communes, forests, grasslands and environmental protection, as well as labor laws and a law on investment by foreigners. These laws should be discussed and adopted through democratic procedures. Meanwhile, the procuratorial and judicial organs should be strengthened. All this will ensure that there are laws to go by, that they are observed and strictly enforced, and that violators are brought to book. The relations between one enterprise and another, between enterprises and the state, between enterprises and individuals and so on should also be defined by law, and many of the contradictions between them should be resolved by law. [1]

In his working report to the Fifteenth Session of the Fifth NPC Standing Committee, Peng Zhen said,

> Economic legislation is becoming increasingly urgent with the development of the four modernizations. Since the Second Session of the Fifth NPC, more than seventy economic laws and regulations have been issued or are being drafted by departments of the State Council, while some other reforms are still in the process of being drafted. Without a lot of experiences in economic legislation China needs more time to fulfill

---

[1] *Selected Works of Deng Xiaoping (1975-1982)* , Foreign Languages Press, Beijing, 1984. p. 158.

the needs of the economy. China issue the laws one by one on the basis of its experience; as one law ripens, one is harvested or issued.

Since then, China's economic legislation has moved on a well-charted course.

Of the fifty-two laws passed by the NPC and its Standing Committee since 1979, twenty-four are economic laws, including the Forest Law of the People's Republic of China (passed in September 1984, and effective from January 1, 1985), the Law on Joint Ventures Involving China-Foreign Investment (passed in July 1979 and effective from July 8, 1979), the Law on Environmental Protection (passed for trial implementation in September 1979 and effective from September 13, 1979), the Regulations on Special Economic Zones in Guangdong Province (endorsed and went into effect on August 26, 1980), the Income Tax Law on Joint Ventures Involving China-Foreign Investment (passed in September 1980 and effective from September 10, 1980), the Private Income Tax Law (passed in September 1980 and effective from September 10, 1980), the Economic Contract Law (passed in December 1981, and effective from July 1, 1982), the Law on Income Tax for Foreign Enterprises in China (passed in December 1981 and effective from January 1, 1982), the Law on Food Sanitation (for trial implementation, passed in November 1982 and taking trial effect on July 1, 1983), the Statistics Law (passed in December 1983 and taking effect on January 1, 1984), the Patent Law (passed in March 1984 and taking effect on April 1, 1985), the Law on Medical Management (passed in September 1984 and taking effect on July 1, 1985), the Accounting Law (passed in January 1985 and taking effect on May 1, 1985), the Law on Economic Contracts Involving Foreign Parties (passed in March 1985 and taking effect on July 1, 1985), the Measurement Law (passed in September 1985 and taking effect on July 1, 1986), the Grasslands Law (passed in September 1985 and taking effect on July 1, 1986), the Fishery Law (passed in January 1986 and taking effect on July 1, 1986), the Law on Foreign Enterprises in China (passed in April 1986 and taking effect on April 12, 1986), and the Land Administration Law (passed in June 1986 and taking effect on January 1, 1987). To enforce these laws, the State Council has issued a large number of economic regulations helping to form an elementary economic legal system in China.

The content of the economic laws may be crystallized into the following points:

— Ensuring the stability and development of social and economic relations and the reasonable exploitation of social wealth and natural resources;

— Boosting the planned commodity economy through a mixture of planning and market mechanisms, and meeting the needs of multi-form economies, multi-form operations and multi-layer economic structures. The laws on taxation and prices, and the Planning Law now being drafted are the ones that will exercise this function;

— Ensuring the smooth implementation of scientific research and development, and the utilization of technologies to raise the scientific and technical level of the country; and

—Invigorating international trade and economic and technical cooperation, and making legal adjustments in international economic relation to boost foreign investment in China under the principle of equality and mutual benefits.

LEGISLATION ON
ECONOMIC ACTIVITIES
INVOLVING FOREIGN PARTIES

Legislation on economic activities involving foreign parties is the legal and specific reflection of China's policies of opening to the outside world, introducing advanced technologies, and protecting the lawful interests of foreign investors. Laws in this field are based on the provisions in Article 18 of the Constitution that "Foreign businesses, other economic bodies and individuals are allowed to invest in China within the purview charted by the law to undertake economic cooperation with Chinese businesses and other economic entities," and that "All their rights and lawful interests are protected by the laws of the People's Republic of China."

Laws such as the Law on Foreign Enterprises in China, the

229

Law on Joint Ventures Involving China-Foreign Investment, and the Law on Income Tax for Foreign Enterprises in China have made definite and specific provisions on the rights and lawful interests of foreign investors, and provide legal guarantees for their business activities in the country.

Their rights in the following areas are:

Investment decisions Overseas investors may decide for themselves the mode, direction, proportion and specific means of their investment in China. In regard to the mode of investment, they may choose among independent enterprise, joint venture, joint operation, processing clients' materials at their demands, compensation trade, lease trade and other flexible forms. Overseas investors have wide areas to invest in. The Regulations on the Implementation of the Law on Joint Ventures Involving China-Foreign Investment alone list twenty-one areas for foreign investment. The percentage of foreign investment in a joint venture is not strictly limited by the laws, but it should not be less than twenty-five percent. Overseas investors may contribute their shares of investment either in the forms of money, equipment and materials, or evaluated industrial property rights and patent technologies.

Management According to Chinese laws, joint ventures are limited companies, in which the two sides share investment, management, profits and losses. Board memberships are divided between the two sides through consultations according to their respective percentage in the total investment. The chairmanship of the board goes to the Chinese side, and the vice-chairmanship belongs to the foreign side. The board handles important matters through consultations between the two parties, and no side should impose its views on the other. Joint ventures are independent in management. The Law on Joint Ventures stipulates in Article 7 that "Joint ventures have the right to manage freely within the scope charted by Chinese laws and the venture's agreements, contracts and rules." Section 2 of Article 56 provides that "Authorities in charge of enterprises and planning do not impose compulsory plans on joint ventures." A joint venture's power of independent management lies in the following areas:

— Deciding its goal of long-term development, plans for

230

short—term production and operation, wage plans and budget;

—Purchasing needed equipment, materials, fuels and components from Chinese or international markets. The prices of exported products may be decided by the joint venture itself and put into the records of the government department in charge and the price regulating department;

—Signing contracts in the capacity of a legal person with other legal persons and economic bodies;

—Establishing its own financial and management systems by the most advanced management methods in the world, and working out its profit-sharing program; and

—Hiring and firing employees, and establishing a system of economic rewards and punishments.

Foreign enterprises in China have more power in management. The Law on Foreign Enterprises in China stipulates in its Article 11 that "Foreign enterprises run freely under their endorsed rules are not subject to interference."

Ownership The Law on Joint Ventures Involving China-Foreign Investment stipulates in Article 2 that "The Chinese Government protects the investment of foreign investors along with profits and other interests that are lawful according to agreements, contracts, and the constitution of the enterprises endorsed by the government." Either party may transfer part or all of its investment to a third party with agreement from the other side and permission from the ratifying authorities. The Law on Foreign Enterprises in China provides in Article 4 that "The investments of foreign investors, profits and other lawful rights in China are protected by Chinese law." Other rights and lawful interests such as trademark and patent rights are protected by the Chinese Government, and no institutions or individuals may encroach upon them.

On the question of nationalization, the Law on Foreign Enterprises in China provides in Article 5 that "The state does not nationalize foreign enterprises. If it has to do so under special circumstances in the interests of the public, it must do so according to legal procedure and make proper compensation."

To facilitate the protection of foreign investment in China, the Chinese Government has signed agreements on investment protection with fourteen countries, and negotiations with other countries on mutual protection of investment have been taking place. The agreements provide clearly that each side shall protect the investment made by the other, and shall not commandeer or nationalize that investment unless it has to do so in the interests of the public. Necessary compensation must then be made.

Profit sharing and remittance The foreign investor in a joint venture has the right to share profits in accordance with his proportion of the registered investment and provisions of the contracts. He can choose either to use the profits as re-investment in China, or remit it abroad in the currency provided by the contract through the Bank of China, and within the scope charted by the Regulations on Foreign Exchange Control. The lawful income of foreign employees in a joint venture may be remitted abroad through the Bank of China after the payment of income tax. The Law on Foreign Enterprises in China stipulates in Article 19 that "Foreign investors may remit abroad the profits, other lawful incomes collected from the business and the funds left after clearing accounts. Foreign employees in foreign businesses may remit their pay and other lawful income abroad after the payment of individual income tax." These measures ensure the interests of foreign investors.

Favored treatment in taxation In line with the Income Tax Law on Joint Ventures Involving China-Foreign Investment, the Individual Income Tax Law and the specific regulations on their implementation, and under the precondition of keeping state sovereignty, the Chinese Government exercises the policy of light taxation through simple procedure to foreign investors. Enterprises involving foreign investment only have to pay income tax, industrial and commercial tax, customs duties, real estate tax, vehicle license-plate tax and a few other local taxes. Moreover, the tax rates are quite low.

To encourage foreign investment, many tax exemptions are practiced. For example, joint ventures with a period of cooperation above twenty years are exempted from taxation for two years from the year they begin to make profits, and are then exempted from half of the taxation for three years. The income tax for foreign businesses, as well as for foreign investors in cooperation with Chinese sides, is a five-grade progressive tax.

232

The tax rate is merely thirty to fifty percent (including local tax). Foreign businesses in low-profit industries are exempted from taxation for one year from the year they begin to collect profits, exempted from half of the taxation for another two years, and then enjoy a tax reduction of fifteen to thirty percent for ten years.

The rate of income tax stands at only fifteen percent for joint ventures, projects of cooperative operation, foreign businesses in the special economic zones, and the same forms of enterprises engaged in production in the fourteen coastal port cities. [1] In a word, the tax rates for foreign investors in China are considerably low.

The right to convenient entrance and departure The Rules on the Implementation of the Law on Joint Ventures Involving China-Foreign Investment stipulate in Article 113 that "The authorities concerned may simplify application procedure for joint venture employees from Hong Kong, Macao and foreign countries (including their dependents) who often enter and leave the country." The simplification saves time for foreign investors and their employees, and enhances business efficiency.

The power to sign contracts Foreign investors may sign contracts in China according to the law and enjoy the rights provided in the contracts. The Law on Economic Contracts Involving Foreign Parties stipulates clearly that a contract has legal power as soon as it takes effect. The two parties must carry out strictly their obligations provided in a contract, and may not unilaterally revise or terminate the contract. The law also stipulates that the ratified contract of a joint venture is not open to the influence of changes in the Chinese laws concerned, and the two sides may abide by the contract until it expires.

The right to litigation The laws of China stipulate that the parties may choose through consultation to solve disputes concerning investment and other economic activities by discussion, mediation, arbitration and litigation. The Rules on the Implementation of the Law on Joint Ventures Involving

---

[1] They are Dalian, Qinhuangdao, Tianjin, Yantai, Qingdao, Lianyungang, Nantong, Shanghai, Ningbo, Wenzhou, Fuzhou, Guangzhou, Zhanjiang and Beihai.

China-Foreign Investment provide in Article 109 that "Both parties in a joint venture should resort to friendly consultation and mediation as much as possible if disputes occur in the implementation of the joint venture's agreement, contract and regulations. When consultation or mediation fails, the two parties should resort to arbitration or judicial judgment." The arbitration body, either Chinese or foreign, is chosen through consultation by the two parties. They can also decide whether to invoke Chinese laws or foreign laws. Some special types of contracts are declared by law to be exceptions. "If a joint venture has no written agreement on arbitration, either of the two parties may file a lawsuit at the people's court of China when a dispute occurs." In the course of litigation, foreign investors and Chinese citizens enjoy equal civil procedural rights. The Civil Procedure Law of the People's Republic of China (for trial implementation) stipulates in Article 186 that "Foreigners and stateless persons enjoy the same rights and shoulder the same duties as Chinese citizens in initiating or defending lawsuits before the people's court. Foreign enterprises and organizations have procedural rights and obligations in lawsuits brought before a Chinese court." These provisions in the procedural laws guarantee the actual rights of foreign investors.

The legal systems of Hong Kong, Macao and Taiwan are completely different from that of the Chinese mainland. Even when they are returned to China in the future, they can have different legal systems as special administrative divisions of China. However, their legal systems will not be presented here.

Index

中国法律制度概述

杜西川
张龄元　著

※

新世界出版社出版
北京外文印刷厂印刷
中国国际图书贸易总公司发行
（中国北京车公庄西路21号）
北京邮政信箱第399号　邮政编码100044
1990年（英）第一版
ISBN 7 - 80005 - 087 - 4／D.001
001000
6 - E - 2347 P